# DK
# ANIMALS

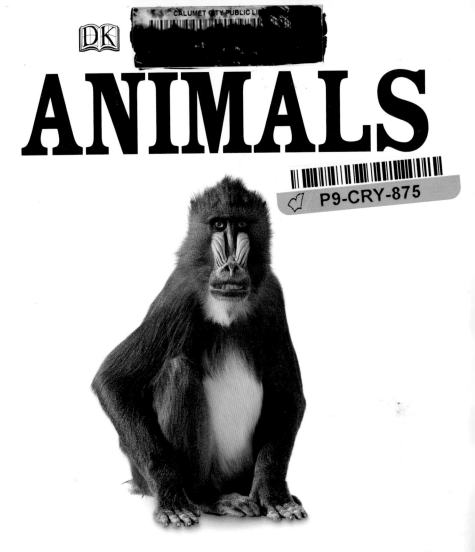

# FACTS AT YOUR FINGERTIPS

LONDON, NEW YORK, MUNICH,
MELBOURNE, and DELHI

**DK DELHI**
**Project editor** Bharti Bedi
**Project art editor** Deep Shikha Walia
**Senior editor** Kingshuk Ghoshal
**Senior art editor** Govind Mittal
**Editors** Nasreen Habib, Neha Chaudhary
**Assistant art editor** Aanchal Singal
**DTP designers** Mohammad Usman, Vishal Bhatia
**Picture researcher** Sumedha Chopra
**Managing editor** Saloni Talwar
**Managing art editor** Romi Chakraborty
**CTS manager** Balwant Singh
**Production manager** Pankaj Sharma

**DK LONDON**
**Senior editor** Dr. Rob Houston
**Senior art editor** Philip Letsu
**US editor** Margaret Parrish
**Jacket editor** Manisha Majithia
**Jacket designer** Laura Brim
**Jacket design development manager**
Sophia Tampakopolous
**Production editor** Ben Marcus
**Production controller** Mary Slater

**Publisher** Andrew Macintyre
**Associate publishing director** Liz Wheeler
**Art director** Phil Ormerod
**Publishing director** Jonathan Metcalf

**Consultant** Dr. Kim Dennis-Bryan

First published in the United States in 2012
by DK Publishing
375 Hudson Street, New York, New York 10014

Copyright © 2012 Dorling Kindersley Limited
12 13 14 15 16  10 9 8 7 6 5 4 3 2 1
001–184267–Jun/12

A catalog record for this book
is available from the Library of Congress.
ISBN: 978-0-7566-9284-1

Printed and bound by South China
Printing Company, China

**Discover more at**
**www.dk.com**

# CONTENTS

**Scales and sizes**
The book contains profiles of animals with scale drawings to show their size.

6 ft (1.8 m)  6 in (15 cm)  1½ in (4 cm)

**Endangered animals**
This label indicates that the animal is in danger of dying out.

ENDANGERED

# Animal kingdom

The animal kingdom is a vast collection of almost 2 million creatures, both weird and wonderful. Members of this group come in many different shapes and sizes, but all have bodies of cells and eat food to get their energy.

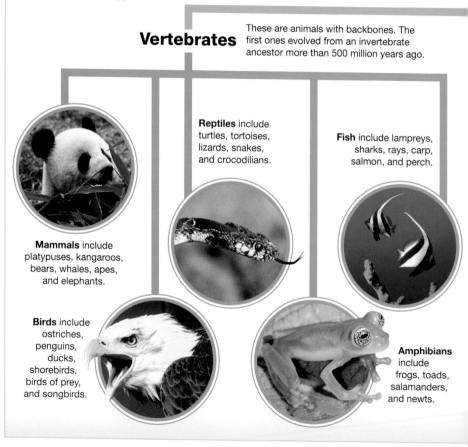

**Vertebrates** These are animals with backbones. The first ones evolved from an invertebrate ancestor more than 500 million years ago.

**Reptiles** include turtles, tortoises, lizards, snakes, and crocodilians.

**Fish** include lampreys, sharks, rays, carp, salmon, and perch.

**Mammals** include platypuses, kangaroos, bears, whales, apes, and elephants.

**Birds** include ostriches, penguins, ducks, shorebirds, birds of prey, and songbirds.

**Amphibians** include frogs, toads, salamanders, and newts.

# Invertebrates

These animals lack a backbone and include a variety of creatures, ranging from sponges and worms, to mollusks, such as this octopus.

The common octopus is an invertebrate

**Arthropods** include insects, centipedes, crabs, spiders, and scorpions.

**Echinoderms** include starfish and their relatives.

**Mollusks** include slugs, snails, octopuses, squid, oysters, and clams.

**Worms** are of many different kinds, including flatworms, roundworms, and segmented worms.

**Cnidarians** are simple animals, including sea anemones, corals, jellyfish, and hydroids.

**Kingdom: Animals**

This is the broadest group that includes all members of a particular kind of organism, such as an animal or a plant. The animal kingdom contains all the animals in the world.

**Phylum: Chordates**

There are 35 smaller groups in the animal kingdom, each called a phylum. The phylum Chordates includes the vertebrates—animals with backbones.

**Class: Mammals**

A class is a major division of a phylum. The mammals form a class of warm-blooded vertebrates. Most mammals give birth to live young.

# Animal species

The animal kingdom contains an amazing variety of creatures. In order to study them better, they are organized into groups. Closely related animals are grouped together. Each animal is identified by a unique two-part label. The first part denotes the animal's genus and the second indicates the species.

## What is a species?

A group of animals that can breed with each other forms a species. There are always some differences between animals of the same species. On the other hand, animals of different species may be very similar. For example, in 1999, scientists noticed that some common pipistrelle bats had a higher-pitched call and only bred among themselves. Although they look almost identical, we now know they form a separate species called the soprano pipistrelle.

**Common pipistrelle**

**Soprano pipistrelle**

### Order: Carnivores
A class is further divided into orders. The order of carnivores contains meat-eating mammals. These animals have special teeth.

### Family: Cats
Every order has families. The cat family includes big cats, such as lions and tigers, as well as small cats, such as bobcats and pumas.

*Felis*

### Genus: Small cats
Families contain genera (plural of genus). The domestic cat belongs to the genus *Felis*, which contains some types of small cat.

### Species: Domestic cat
The domestic cat belongs to the species *silvestris*. It is a descendant of the wildcat and has spread all over the world, living in most human settlements. Scientists call it *Felis silvestris*.

*Felis silvestris*

# Evolution

Living organisms may change over many generations in a process called evolution. It is driven mainly by natural selection—animals better suited to survive leave more offspring and pass on to those offspring the characteristics that help them survive.

## Natural selection

Some animals inherit certain features from their parents that increase their chances of survival. Those that survive have offspring of their own and pass on their useful features. These offspring are also able to survive better. This happens over many generations and may result in a major change in the species.

**Color that camouflages a moth better will be passed on to the next generation**

## Elephant evolution

Every life-form on the Earth today has evolved over millions of years from ancestors that looked very different. Elephants evolved from an unknown ancestor similar to *Moeritherium*, which lived 37 million years ago and looked more like a hippopotamus.

*Gomphotherium*

*Phioma*

*Moeritherium*

## Adaptation

Most animals are adapted to live and reproduce in the environment in which they live—some better than others. The colors of the Argentine horned frog help it blend in among leaf litter.

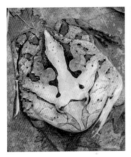

**Argentine horned frog camouflaged in leaf litter**

## Extinction

An animal becomes extinct because it cannot adapt quickly enough to the changes in its environment. Around 65 million years ago, an asteroid or comet hit the Earth, triggering a series of environmental changes that led to the extinction of the dinosaurs.

*Coelophysis,* a dinosaur

African savanna elephant

*Deinotherium*

# Domestic animals

A domestic animal is one that is taken into human care. All animals that have been domesticated today, including dogs, cats, and cattle, were once wild. Over many generations, humans learned to change the bodies and behavior of many of these animals by controlling which animals breed. This process of selective breeding is known as artificial selection.

**Camel** pulls cart along a paved road

## Workers

Humans value animals for their natural abilities, such as strength. Horses and camels, for example, are used as "mounts"—people ride them for transportation. "Pack" animals, such as donkeys and mules, help carry goods on their back. "Draft" animals, such as heavy horses, pull carts and sleds.

# WHERE DO THEY COME FROM?

Humans have domesticated a number of animals for transportation, food, and companionship. Many domestic animals have ancestors whose behavior changed over generations due to human control. The dog was the first animal to be tamed, at least 15,000 years ago.

### DOG
**Ancestor:** Gray wolf
**Date:** Domesticated between 30,000 BCE and 13,000 BCE
**Purpose:** Hunting and companionship

### CATTLE
**Ancestor:** Aurochs
**Date:** Domesticated around 6,000 BCE
**Purpose:** Meat, milk, leather, and pulling carts

### CHICKEN
**Ancestor:** Red jungle-fowl
**Date:** Domesticated some time before 6,000 BCE
**Purpose:** Meat, eggs, and feathers

### HONEY BEE
**Ancestor:** Genus *Apis*
**Date:** Domesticated around 3,000 BCE
**Purpose:** Honey, wax, and pollination

### COCHINEAL INSECT
**Ancestor:** Cochineal insect
**Date:** Domesticated around 2,000 BCE
**Purpose:** Red dye

### GOLDFISH
**Ancestor:** Asian carp
**Date:** Domesticated before 1,000 CE
**Purpose:** Decoration and companionship

# Mammals

Mammals are warm-blooded animals, which means that they can maintain a constant body temperature and stay active whatever the weather. Most suckle milk during their early lives. They are widespread around the planet. From apes to elephants, many mammals display complex social behavior, including play—a means of learning and bonding between the young of some mammals.

**MARINE MAMMAL**
The bottlenosed dolphin has adapted to a life in water. But like other mammals, it breathes air, so must visit the surface every few minutes.

# Mammals

These vertebrates feed their young on milk from the female's mammary glands, which give the group its name. Most give birth to live young, while a handful of mammals lay eggs. All mammals grow body hair at some point in their lives.

Most **primates,** such as these orangutans, carry their young with them until they are old enough to fend for themselves

## Parenting

Many mammals spend a lot of time and energy bringing up their young. A mammal's first food is its mother's milk, which contains all the nourishment the young one needs.

# Types of mammal

There are three types of mammal: the egg-laying monotremes; the pouched mammals, or marsupials; and the placentals. Most mammals belong to the third group.

**Placentals** give birth to live young. They start growing inside the mother, being nourished via a structure called the placenta.

There are only five species of **monotreme.** The short-nosed echidna is one of them.

**Marsupials** give birth at an early stage of the young's development. They are nurtured by the mother's milk inside a pouch attached to her body.

# Hair

Hair is unique to mammals. A hairy coat helps maintain a constant body temperature. In cold conditions, each hair is pulled upright, trapping a layer of air near the skin and keeping the mammal warm. It also waterproofs and protects the skin.

Hair **above skin** is dead

**Erector** muscle

Living **root of hair** grows from follicle, or base

**Blood supply** to follicle

# SPECIAL ADAPTATIONS

**Bats are the only mammals that can fly**

**A bat's wings** are formed from a double layer of skin stretched between the bones of the fingers and arm.

**Marine mammals**, such as whales, dolphins, and porpoises, evolved from land-dwelling ancestors that took to water. They have flippers instead of arms or legs.

# Monotremes and marsupials

Monotremes are the only egg-laying mammals. Marsupials are born at an early stage of development and most complete it in the mother's pouch, nourished by milk.

## FOCUS ON...
## YOUNG

Marsupials such as opossums need time to develop before leaving their mother.

▲ Newborn babies remain attached to the mother's nipples inside the pouch. They feed on her milk.

▲ As they grow older, the young ones cling to their mother's back using well-developed claws.

▲ After a few months, the young ones spend more and more time outside their mother's pouch, returning at the first sign of danger.

### Short-nosed echidna
*Tachyglossus aculeatus*

Also called the spiny anteater, this monotreme has long spines on its body. It often finds its prey by using the sensors on its long snout, which detect electrical signals emitted from the bodies of its victims.

| | |
|---|---|
| **SIZE** | 12–18 in (30–45 cm) long |
| **DIET** | Ants, termites, grubs, and worms |
| **HABITAT** | Forests, deserts, and open habitats |
| **DISTRIBUTION** | Australia and New Guinea |

## Koala
*Phascolarctos cinereus*

Although it has a large, wide, bearlike face, the koala is not related to bears. It is a marsupial and female koalas have a pouch in which they carry their young. Koalas feed at night, eating about 1 lb (500 g) of eucalyptus leaves, and they doze during the day.

**SIZE**  26–32¼ in (65–82 cm) long

**DIET**  Mainly eucalyptus leaves

**HABITAT**  Forests

**DISTRIBUTION**  Eastern Australia

## Duck-billed platypus
*Ornithorhynchus anatinus*

The duck-billed platypus is a monotreme and has webbed feet that help it to swim. The male platypus uses a poisonous spur on its hind foot to kill prey.

*Ducklike bill*

**SIZE**  16–23½ in (40–60 cm) long

**DIET**  Invertebrates

**HABITAT**  Rivers and streams

**DISTRIBUTION**  Eastern Australia and Tasmania

## Red kangaroo
*Macropus rufus*

When fleeing from danger, this marsupial bounds on its strong hind legs. It is the largest and swiftest kangaroo and can reach speeds of more than 30 mph (50 kph).

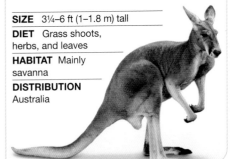

**SIZE**  3¼–6 ft (1–1.8 m) tall

**DIET**  Grass shoots, herbs, and leaves

**HABITAT**  Mainly savanna

**DISTRIBUTION**  Australia

# Insect-eaters

Moles, shrews, hedgehogs, armadillos, tenrecs, sengis, and aardvarks belong to several unrelated groups of mammal, but they all devour insects. Most of them have a long snout and a keen sense of smell.

FOCUS ON...
## FINDING FOOD
Insect-eaters look for food using various senses and body parts.

## Aardvark
*Orycteropus afer*

A swift burrower, the aardvark uses its shovel-like claws to rip open termite nests. It then inserts its sticky tongue and laps up the insects. Strands of long white hair and small folds of skin in its nostrils filter out dust.

**SIZE** 3¼–4¼ ft (1–1.3 m) long

**DIET** Ants and termites

**HABITAT** Savanna and scrublands

**DISTRIBUTION** South of the Sahara Desert in Africa

## Western European hedgehog
*Erinaceus europaeus*

Covered with spines, this hedgehog curls up into a prickly ball when alarmed. It hibernates in winter—lowering both its body temperature and heart rate to do so.

**SIZE** 8–12 in (20–30 cm) long

**DIET** Small animals, birds' eggs, and carrion

**HABITAT** Woodlands, farmlands, and gardens

**DISTRIBUTION** Western Europe

▲ The sengi locates food using its long, flexible snout and by digging with its claws.

▲ Giant anteaters rip open termite nests with their sharp claws before starting to snack.

▲ They are almost blind, so golden moles detect vibrations in sand to find insects.

▲ An aardvark uses its senses of smell and acute hearing to hunt for ants to feed on.

## European mole
*Talpa europaea*

With fur as smooth as silk, the European mole moves easily as it digs tunnels in the soil. Almost blind, it uses its hind feet for support and its front legs to scoop soil to either side of its body.

**SIZE** 4½–6½ in (11–16 cm) long

**DIET** Worms and other soil animals

**HABITAT** Meadows, pastures, gardens, and parks

**DISTRIBUTION** Europe to northern Asia

## Eurasian shrew
*Sorex araneus*

This voracious eater consumes 80–90 percent of its body weight in food in a day. The shrew's pointed, flexible snout helps it sniff out insects and worms. Despite being one of the smallest mammals, the shrew is aggressive and territorial.

**SIZE** 2¼–3¼ in (5.5–8 cm) long

**DIET** Insects, worms, and carrion

**HABITAT** Woodlands and grasslands

**DISTRIBUTION** Europe to northern Asia

## Bushveld sengi
*Elephantulus intufi*

Sengis were once known as elephant shrews, due to their long, flexible snout. They live in pairs and occupy territories, defending them against rivals.

**SIZE**  3½–4½ in (9–11 cm) long

**DIET**  Insects, spiders, and earthworms

**HABITAT**  Steppe grasslands and semi-deserts

**DISTRIBUTION**  Southern Africa

## Six-banded armadillo
*Euphractus sexcinctus*

Hair grows between plates

Bands of tough plates form armor

## Giant anteater
*Myrmecophaga tridactyla*

With its large front claws, this anteater rips open ant and termite nests easily. When walking, the giant anteater moves on its knuckles with its claws folded underneath. This juvenile individual does not yet have a full-length snout.

**SIZE**  3¼–6½ ft (1–2 m) long

**DIET**  Ants, termites, and other insects

**HABITAT**  Forests and grasslands

**DISTRIBUTION**  Central to South America

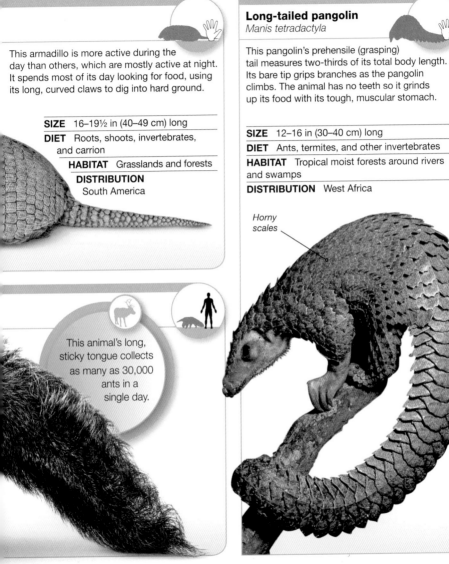

This armadillo is more active during the day than others, which are mostly active at night. It spends most of its day looking for food, using its long, curved claws to dig into hard ground.

**SIZE**  16–19½ in (40–49 cm) long

**DIET**  Roots, shoots, invertebrates, and carrion

**HABITAT**  Grasslands and forests

**DISTRIBUTION**  South America

This animal's long, sticky tongue collects as many as 30,000 ants in a single day.

## Long-tailed pangolin
*Manis tetradactyla*

This pangolin's prehensile (grasping) tail measures two-thirds of its total body length. Its bare tip grips branches as the pangolin climbs. The animal has no teeth so it grinds up its food with its tough, muscular stomach.

**SIZE**  12–16 in (30–40 cm) long

**DIET**  Ants, termites, and other invertebrates

**HABITAT**  Tropical moist forests around rivers and swamps

**DISTRIBUTION**  West Africa

Horny scales

## FOCUS ON...
# DIET

Bats are active at night when they look for fruits, insects, and even blood.

▲ The vampire bat's saliva numbs the skin of its victims so they can't feel the bat's bite.

▲ Many fruit bats have a long tongue that helps them to collect nectar and pollen.

▲ Most bats can catch insects in midair and find prey in the dark.

# Bats

Bats are the only mammals that can fly. Their wings are formed from skin stretched between the side of the body, arm, and the four long fingers on each hand. While flying, most bats emit chirps that reflect off prey, and the echoes help the bats find their victims.

### Vampire bat
*Desmodus rotundus*

The vampire bat is the only mammal that feeds entirely on blood. It approaches its prey silently and uses its bladelike incisor teeth to cut into the flesh. Its saliva prevents the prey's blood from clotting while it feeds.

| | |
|---|---|
| **SIZE** | 2¾–3¾ in (7–9.5 cm) long |
| **DIET** | Blood of birds, tapirs, or farm animals |
| **HABITAT** | Roosts in trees, caves, mines, or old buildings |
| **DISTRIBUTION** | Central and South America |

## Brown long-eared bat
*Plecotus auritus*

This bat's huge ears are good for picking up sounds made by prey, but it also hunts by echolocation—listening for echoes of its chirps.

**SIZE** 1½–2 in (4–5 cm) long

**DIET** Insects, including moths and beetles

**HABITAT** Woodlands, caves, mines, and cellars

**DISTRIBUTION** Europe and central Asia

## Lesser horseshoe bat
*Rhinolophus hipposideros*

This bat's central body is smaller than a human thumb. A growth on its nose, called a nose-leaf, focuses the chirps it makes and helps it find insects.

**SIZE** 1½–1¾ in (3.5–4.5 cm) long

**DIET** Small flying insects

**HABITAT** Woodlands and scrublands

**DISTRIBUTION** Europe, Africa, and western Asia

## Spectacled flying fox
*Pteropus conspicillatus*

Fruit bats use their eyesight and sense of smell to locate food. They have claws on both their thumb and second finger. This fruit bat has a ring of pale yellow fur around each eye.

The spectacled flying fox can travel as far as 45 miles (70 km) in search of food.

**SIZE** 9–10 in (22–25 cm) long

**DIET** Fruits and flowers

**HABITAT** Tropical rainforests

**DISTRIBUTION** Indonesia's Moluccan Islands, New Guinea, and northeastern Australia

# Primates

Lemurs, monkeys, and apes make up most of this group. Most kinds of primate live in tropical rainforests and form families or social groups. Primates have grasping hands and feet that are useful for climbing trees or handling tools. Some primates are remarkably intelligent.

## Ring-tailed lemur
*Lemur catta*

This lemur likes company and lives in large groups of up to 25 animals. Females take charge of the group. Unlike most lemurs, this one is active during the day and feeds on the ground.

**SIZE** 20–23½ in (51–60 cm) long

**DIET** Fruits

**HABITAT** Rainforests

**DISTRIBUTION** Eastern Madagascar

## Philippine tarsier
*Tarsius syrichta*

Of all mammals, Philippine tarsiers have the largest eyes relative to their body size. They sleep in dark hollows during the day and venture out to hunt at night. Their huge eyes help them to see well in the dark.

**SIZE** 3–6½ in (8.5–16 cm) long

**DIET** Insects

**HABITAT** Rainforests and scrublands

**DISTRIBUTION** Philippines

## Common marmoset
*Callithrix jacchus*

This unusual monkey has clawlike nails that help it cling vertically to tree trunks and run on all fours along branches. It is one of the "New World monkeys," meaning it lives in the Americas.

**SIZE** 4¾–6 in (12–15 cm) long

**DIET** Fruits, flowers, nectar, and small animals

**HABITAT** Forests

**DISTRIBUTION** Northeastern Brazil

# Mandrill

*Mandrillus sphinx*

The largest monkeys in the world, mandrills spend most of their time on the ground looking for food. They only climb trees to sleep at night. Males yawn widely when threatened, displaying their fearsome teeth.

**SIZE** 25–32 in (63–81 cm) long

**DIET** Fruits, eggs, and small animals

**HABITAT** Rainforests

**DISTRIBUTION** West central Africa

Scarlet nose and blue ridges on the face are unique to mandrills

Mandrill troops may have more than 100 members.

Long, powerful arms

# Like humans,

**Japanese macaques can develop different accents depending on where they live**

## JAPANESE MACAQUES

Japanese macaques, also called snow monkeys, have several types of behavior that remind us of humans. Many take a dip in hot springs to keep themselves warm, and others have been seen washing mud off their food, even seasoning it by dipping it in seawater.

# Rodents and rabbits

Rodents are found worldwide and have long tails and a pair of incisor teeth specialized for gnawing. Rabbits, and their relatives hares and pikas, share many features with rodents but have a lighter skull and a second set of incisors that are set directly behind the first pair.

## Crested porcupine
*Hystrix cristata*

The spines of porcupines are actually hair made up of keratin—a substance also found in horns and nails. The crested porcupine often raises its sharp spines when threatened, warning predators about a painful jab.

**SIZE** 23½–40 in (60–100 cm) long

**DIET** Fruits and carrion

**HABITAT** Savanna grasslands, forests, and rocky terrain

**DISTRIBUTION** Northern Africa, as far south as Tanzania

## Eastern gray squirrel
*Sciurus carolinensis*

The eastern gray squirrel spread from North America to parts of Europe, where it is now replacing the native red squirrel. This agile animal has an active memory that helps it to locate food hoarded previously.

**SIZE**  9–12 in (23–30 cm) long

**DIET**  Nuts, seeds, flowers, and fruits

**HABITAT**  Forests and urban areas

**DISTRIBUTION**  Canada and United States; introduced to Europe

## Naked mole-rat
*Heterocephalus glaber*

This bizarre rodent lives underground in huge communal burrows. Its social system is unique among mammals, with only one dominant female, or the "queen," producing pups.

**SIZE**  3¼–4 in (8–10 cm) long

**DIET**  Roots, bulbs, and underground plant parts

**HABITAT**  Deserts and semi-deserts

**DISTRIBUTION**  East Africa

## Brown rat
*Rattus norvegicus*

Brown rats have a keen sense of smell, and they can smell food more than 2 miles (3 km) away while foraging at night. Rats in a pack find each other by smell.

**SIZE**  8½–11½ in (21–29 cm) long

**DIET**  Almost anything

**HABITAT**  Grasslands and urban areas

**DISTRIBUTION**  Worldwide, except polar regions

## European hare
*Lepus europaeus*

These hares live alone and are active at night. However, in spring they gather for a "boxing" courtship where females fight off males until they are ready to mate.

**SIZE**  19–28 in (48–70 cm) long

**DIET**  Grass, herbs, bark, and rarely carrion

**HABITAT**  Open woods, bush, and grasslands

**DISTRIBUTION**  Europe; introduced to Australia, New Zealand, and North America

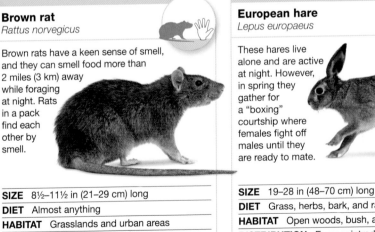

# Carnivores

The carnivores, meaning meat-eaters, are grouped together not because they are all predators, although most of them are, but because they are all related. Most carnivores are fast runners with flexible spines and sharp teeth that help them tear flesh.

## FOCUS ON...
## HUNTING

Most cats are lone hunters that use stealth tactics to catch prey, while dogs chase prey in a group.

▲ A tiger stalks its prey. It gets as close as possible to its prey and then gives it a short chase to get close enough to pounce.

▲ Wild dogs hunt in packs, which allows them to catch prey larger than themselves. They run down prey in a long-distance endurance chase.

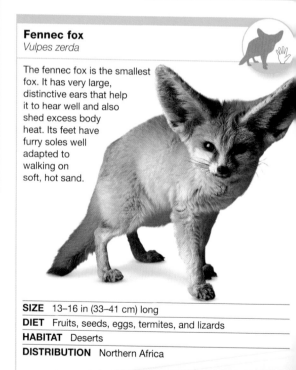

**Fennec fox**
*Vulpes zerda*

The fennec fox is the smallest fox. It has very large, distinctive ears that help it to hear well and also shed excess body heat. Its feet have furry soles well adapted to walking on soft, hot sand.

| | |
|---|---|
| **SIZE** | 13–16 in (33–41 cm) long |
| **DIET** | Fruits, seeds, eggs, termites, and lizards |
| **HABITAT** | Deserts |
| **DISTRIBUTION** | Northern Africa |

## Polar bear
*Ursus maritimus*

One of the largest land predators, a polar bear has a keen sense of smell and can detect seals from about half a mile (1 km) away, even when the seals are hidden in their birth lairs underneath 3¼ ft (1 m) of hardened snow.

**SIZE** 6–9 ft (1.8–2.8 m) long

**DIET** Seals, birds' eggs, lemmings, mosses, and carrion, such as caribou and musk oxen

**HABITAT** Arctic ice fields

**DISTRIBUTION** Arctic Ocean and polar parts of Russia, Alaska, Canada, Norway, and Greenland

## Gray wolf
*Canis lupus*

The largest member of the dog family, the gray wolf forms packs to hunt animals. As a group, they can take down prey as large as a bison. Packs are led by a dominant pair.

**SIZE** 3–5¼ ft (0.9–1.6 m) long

**DIET** Animals, such as beavers, hares, and moose

**HABITAT** Forests, tundra, deserts, and mountains

**DISTRIBUTION** North America, Greenland, Europe, and Asia

## Red panda
*Ailurus fulgens*

The red panda has claws that can be partly drawn in. It is a good climber. Active mainly during the night, it communicates by making shrill cries, whistles, and squeaks. It marks its territory with urine, droppings, and a musklike scent.

**SIZE** 20–29 in (50–73 cm) long

**DIET** Plant matter, birds' eggs and chicks, small mammals, and birds

**HABITAT** Dense temperate mountain forests

**DISTRIBUTION** Himalayas

## Lion
*Panthera leo*

Lions are the only cats that live in groups, called prides. They are often seen napping under trees. Since they have no natural predators, they are perfectly safe sleeping in the open.

**SIZE** 5¼–8¼ ft (1.6–2.5 m) long

**DIET** Large animals, such as zebras, impalas, and buffalos

**HABITAT** Tropical forests, savanna, and deserts

**DISTRIBUTION** Africa and India

## Sea otter
*Enhydra lutris*

The smallest marine mammal, the sea otter lives at sea for most of its life and comes ashore rarely. It feeds on clams, which it breaks open with a stone that it carries around with it.

**SIZE** 2½–4 ft (0.75–1.2 m) long

**DIET** Fish and clams

**HABITAT** Kelp forests

**DISTRIBUTION** North Pacific

## Leopard
*Panthera pardus*

This cat is an adept climber and often spies on its prey from high in trees. Using its immense strength, this animal drags its kill up the tree to keep it from being stolen.

**SIZE** 3–6¼ ft (0.9–1.9 m) long

**DIET** Small antelopes

**HABITAT** Forests, mountains, deserts, and grasslands

**DISTRIBUTION** Africa and southern Asia

# Caracal
*Caracal caracal*

The caracal can spring and jump exceptionally well, sometimes as high as 10 ft (3 m). Amazingly, it can snatch a flying bird with its paw. It is also called the desert lynx.

**SIZE** 2–3½ ft (0.6–1.06 m) long

**DIET** Rodents and small animals

**HABITAT** Dry scrublands

**DISTRIBUTION** Africa and Asia

# Least weasel
*Mustela nivalis*

The least weasel has a chestnut coat that turns white in winter. This helps it to blend in better with its snowy home. Its small, flattened head is ideal for entering mouse burrows.

**SIZE** 4¼–10 in (11–26 cm) long

**DIET** Mainly mice

**HABITAT** Forests, mountains, grasslands, and Arctic tundra

**DISTRIBUTION** North America, Europe, and northern, central, and eastern Asia

Despite being the smallest carnivore, the least weasel can kill a rabbit 10 times its own weight.

At up to 675 lb (300 kg), the Siberian tiger is the world's heaviest cat, weighing as much as

# four adult men

**SIBERIAN TIGER**
The Siberian tiger is the subspecies living in the cold climate of far eastern Russia and nothernmost China. This cat has evolved a thick fur coat and layer of fat around its belly and flanks, which help to keep it warm in the low Siberian temperatures. The animal seen here is an immature male.

## Raccoon
*Procyon lotor*

Raccoons are smart enough to open doors and latches using their agile front paws when looking for food. They are also known to rub their food clean or rinse it before eating.

**SIZE** 17½–24½ in (44–62 cm) long

**DIET** Fruits, small mammals, and invertebrates

**HABITAT** Mainly woodlands and scrublands

**DISTRIBUTION** South Canada to Central America

## Striped skunk
*Mephitis mephitis*

Skunks spray a nasty smelling liquid if threatened. The odor of the spray is so strong that people can smell it from half a mile (1 km) away. The striped skunk likes to live alone, but may come together in groups in winter burrows.

**SIZE** 9–16 in (23–40 cm) long

**DIET** Small animals, such as mice, squirrels, frogs, and insects; also garbage

**HABITAT** Forests and open habitats

**DISTRIBUTION** Canada to Mexico

## Meerkat
*Suricata suricatta*

These friendly mongooses live in groups. When a group is out hunting during the day, some meerkats stand guard. They warn the group if a predator is nearby. All the group then dives for cover.

**SIZE** 9½–14 in (24–35 cm) long

**DIET** Mainly insects and scorpions

**HABITAT** Deserts and semi-deserts

**DISTRIBUTION** Southern Africa

## Walrus
*Odobenus rosmarus*

This enormous seal uses its tusks to haul itself out of water. The tusks are actually teeth that can grow up to 3¼ ft (1 m). The male walrus also uses its tusks to compete for mates.

**SIZE**   7½–12 ft (2.3–3.6 m) long

**DIET**   Clams and eels

**HABITAT**   Shallow seas

**DISTRIBUTION**
Arctic Ocean

## Common seal
*Phoca vitulina*

Also called the harbor seal, the common seal does not travel more than 12 miles (19 km) out to sea from the shore. Like other true seals, but unlike walruses and sea lions, it cannot use its flippers to move on land. The flippers propel it with speed and agility in water.

**SIZE**   4–6½ ft (1.2–2 m) long

**DIET**   Mainly fish

**HABITAT**   Temperate coasts

**DISTRIBUTION**   North Atlantic and North Pacific

# Elephants

Elephants are the largest land animals. They live in close-knit family groups led by the oldest female. These animals have pillarlike legs, large ears, a mobile trunk, and specialized incisor teeth in the form of tusks. They can live for as long as 70 years.

## African savanna elephant
*Loxodonta africana*

This is the largest of the three elephant species. A single adult eats around 300 lb (135 kg) of food a day. These elephants have forward-curving tusks that are sometimes used to loosen mineral-rich soil that is then eaten for the salt.

**SIZE** 10–12 ft (3–3.6 m) tall

**DIET** Bark, leaves, and grass

**HABITAT** Grasslands, deserts, mountains, and rainforests

**DISTRIBUTION** Africa

## Asiatic elephant
*Elephas maximus*

Asiatic elephants have smaller ears than African elephants. Their numbers are rapidly dwindling because their forest homes are being destroyed. Fewer than 60,000 of these elephants may be alive today. These animals have small tusks that may be absent in the females.

**SIZE**  6½–12 ft (2–3.6 m) tall

**DIET**  Bark, leaves, and grass

**HABITAT**  Savanna and open forests

**DISTRIBUTION**  Southern and southeast Asia

*Five toenails on each forefoot and four on each hind foot*

## African forest elephant
*Loxodonta cyclotis*

Some experts think this elephant is part of the same species as the African savanna elephant, while others regard it as a separate species. In addition to being smaller, it has darker skin and more rounded ears. Its tusks are relatively straight and point downward, helping the elephant to move freely in dense vegetation.

**SIZE**  6½–8¼ ft (2–2.5 m) tall

**DIET**  Barks, leaves, branches, grass, and fruits

**HABITAT**  Deep rainforests

**DISTRIBUTION**  West and central Africa

# Hoofed mammals

Mammals with hooves fall into two natural groups, the odd-toed horses and rhinos and the even-toed pigs, deer, antelopes, and relatives. These plant-eaters have grinding cheek teeth and specialized intestines.

FOCUS ON...
## TOES
The number of toes is the key feature defining the different hoofed animal groups.

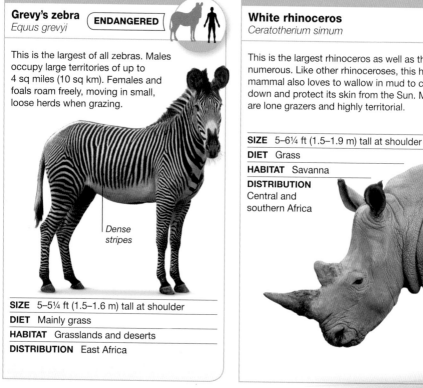

### Grevy's zebra
*Equus grevyi*   `ENDANGERED`

This is the largest of all zebras. Males occupy large territories of up to 4 sq miles (10 sq km). Females and foals roam freely, moving in small, loose herds when grazing.

Dense stripes

| | |
|---|---|
| **SIZE** | 5–5¼ ft (1.5–1.6 m) tall at shoulder |
| **DIET** | Mainly grass |
| **HABITAT** | Grasslands and deserts |
| **DISTRIBUTION** | East Africa |

### White rhinoceros
*Ceratotherium simum*

This is the largest rhinoceros as well as the most numerous. Like other rhinoceroses, this hoofed mammal also loves to wallow in mud to cool down and protect its skin from the Sun. Males are lone grazers and highly territorial.

| | |
|---|---|
| **SIZE** | 5–6¼ ft (1.5–1.9 m) tall at shoulder |
| **DIET** | Grass |
| **HABITAT** | Savanna |
| **DISTRIBUTION** | Central and southern Africa |

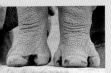

▲ Three toes on each foot of a rhinoceros help bear its weight.

▲ A hoof covers the single toe on each foot of a horse.

▲ A pig has four toes, of which the two larger ones bear its weight.

▲ A deer's foot is like a pig's, but the pair of smaller toes are shorter.

This rhinoceros gets its name from the Afrikaans word *weit*, meaning "wide"—a reference to its mouth.

### Warthog
*Phacochoerus africanus*

This wild pig species uses its tough teeth or lips to nip off grass, and roots for juicy underground stems with its snout.

**SIZE** 25–33½ in (64–85 cm) tall at shoulder

**DIET** Grass and underground stems

**HABITAT** Open woodlands, savanna, and scrublands

**DISTRIBUTION** South of the Sahara in Africa

## Axis deer
*Axis axis*

Known as "chital" in Asia, the axis deer lives in large herds of 100 or more, including males, females, and young.

**SIZE** 23½–40 in (60–100 cm) tall at shoulder

**DIET** Variety of plants

**HABITAT** Deciduous forests

**DISTRIBUTION** South Asia; introduced to Australia and North America

## Hippopotamus
*Hippopotamus amphibius*

This is the larger of the only two species of hippo living today. The body of a hippo is slightly heavier than water. This allows it to walk on the riverbed when completely submerged. It can hold its breath under water for up to 5 minutes.

**SIZE** 4¼–5½ ft (1.3–1.7 m) tall at shoulder

**DIET** Mainly grass

**HABITAT** Wetlands and rivers

**DISTRIBUTION** Eastern, western, and southern Africa

## Impala
*Aepyceros melampus*

Impalas are graceful and adaptable antelopes. When in danger, they emit loud warning snorts and race off in a zigzag, interspersed with leaps to confuse predators.

**SIZE** 29–36 in (73–92 cm) tall at shoulder

**DIET** Mainly grass

**HABITAT** Open habitats

**DISTRIBUTION** East and southern Africa

## Alpine ibex
*Capra ibex*

The alpine ibex lives above the treeline in the Alps. It has thick, curved horns up to 3¼ ft (1 m) long. Males compete for the attention of the females by fighting.

**SIZE** 20–40 in (50–100 cm) tall at shoulder

**DIET** Grass, buds, and shoots

**HABITAT** Open, rocky mountains

**DISTRIBUTION** The Alps of Europe

## Giraffe
*Giraffa camelopardalis*

An elongated neck, tongue, and shoulders allow the giraffe to browse higher than any other mammal. Giraffes have large eyes and ears, stiltlike legs, heavy feet, and a thin tail with a long black tuft that helps to whisk flies away.

**SIZE** 14¾–18 ft (4.5–5.5 m)

**DIET** Mainly acacia leaves and wild apricot

**HABITAT** Dry savanna and open woodlands

**DISTRIBUTION** Africa

Despite having the longest neck, giraffes have only seven neck vertebrae, as in most other mammals.

## Bactrian camel  (ENDANGERED)
*Camelus bactrianus*

Summer coat

A thick, brown coat covers the two-humped Bactrian camel in the cold Gobi Desert winters. The animal sheds this shaggy coat in spring.

**SIZE** 6–7½ ft (1.8–2.3 m) tall at shoulder

**DIET** Grass, leaves, and shrubs

**HABITAT** Deserts, steppes, and rocky plains

**DISTRIBUTION** Gobi Desert, central Asia

# Cetaceans

Whales, dolphins, and porpoises make up an order of mammals called the cetaceans. They are divided into those that have teeth and those that have plates made of baleen instead. Like land mammals, cetaceans breathe using their lungs and suckle their young. They are found throughout the world's oceans.

## Sperm whale
*Physeter catodon*

The huge square head of a sperm whale is filled mostly with waxy oils. When cold, the wax hardens, which may help the whale control its buoyancy. These whales hold the record for diving deeper than any other mammal. They can go as far down as 10,200 ft (3,100 m). Sperm whales usually dive for about 40–50 minutes.

The sperm whale is the largest living toothed animal on the Earth.

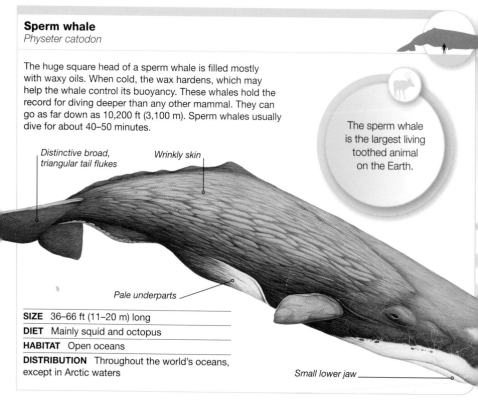

*Distinctive broad, triangular tail flukes*

*Wrinkly skin*

*Pale underparts*

*Small lower jaw*

**SIZE** 36–66 ft (11–20 m) long

**DIET** Mainly squid and octopus

**HABITAT** Open oceans

**DISTRIBUTION** Throughout the world's oceans, except in Arctic waters

# Killer whale
*Orcinus orca*

Killer whales, or orcas, are in fact huge dolphins. They are efficient predators that hunt in pods, chasing down and herding fish. They may even almost beach themselves on shores to catch seals or sea lions.

*Dorsal fin in males is taller and less curved than in females*

*Large, paddle-shaped flippers*

**SIZE** 18–33 ft (5.5–10 m) long

**DIET** Fish, seals, sharks, other cetaceans

**HABITAT** Coastal areas, seas, and oceans

**DISTRIBUTION** Throughout the world's oceans, except under polar ice

---

# Humpback whale
*Megaptera novaeangliae*

These whales have long baleen plates that hang from their upper jaws and feed by filtering food from the water. Humpback whales sing to attract mates or find other whales.

**SIZE** 39–49 ft (12–15 m) long

**DIET** Mainly krill and fish

**HABITAT** Coastal areas, seas, and oceans

**DISTRIBUTION** Worldwide, except the Mediterranean Sea, Black Sea, Caspian Sea, Red Sea, and some Arctic waters

---

# Amazon River dolphin
*Inia geoffrensis*

This freshwater dolphin is curious and may approach boats or swimmers. A long beak and a flexible neck help it to poke around on the riverbed for prey. It has a hump on its back in place of a dorsal fin.

**SIZE** 6–8¼ft (1.8–2.5 m) long

**DIET** Crabs, river turtles, and armored catfish

**HABITAT** Rivers

**DISTRIBUTION** South America

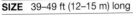

# Birds

Birds are the most accomplished of all flying vertebrates. Most birds can fly, and this ability has helped them to spread across the world, even to remote islands and polar regions. Like mammals, birds are warm-blooded, but they reproduce by laying eggs. Birds use beaks—toothless jaws that are lightweight but strong—for feeding and preening.

**NESTING**
Most birds build nests to protect their eggs and young. Carmine bee-eaters dig burrows in vertical sandbanks along rivers.

# Birds

Birds are warm-blooded, egg-laying vertebrates. Most birds can fly, thanks to their unique features, including lightweight, hollow bones, a light, toothless beak, and feathered wings.

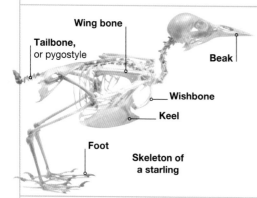

**Wing bone**

**Tailbone,** or pygostyle

**Beak**

**Wishbone**

**Keel**

**Foot**

**Skeleton of a starling**

## Anatomy

Birds are adapted in ways that make them good at flying. Most of their bones are hollow, reducing body weight. The giant keel on the breastbone anchors their large, powerful flight muscles. These can form up to 40 percent of the total body weight in some birds. The wishbone functions like a spring when the wings beat up and down.

## Types of feather

Of all living animals, only birds have feathers, which are formed from the same material as mammal hair—keratin. In addition to being used for flying, feathers also protect birds from heat and cold and keep them dry. Flying birds have four types of feather—down, contour, tail, and flight.

**Down feathers** are soft, and form a warm underlayer.

**Contour feathers** provide a smooth cover over the body.

**Tail feathers** help mainly in flight but many males use them in display.

**Flight feathers** provide the lift needed for flying.

## Flight styles

Birds flutter, swoop, glide, or soar overhead depending on their wing shape. Owls have broad wings that they beat slowly. Woodpeckers flap their broad, tapering wings in bursts. Parrot wings are typically narrow and pointed, enabling them to fly at high speeds.

**Nest** woven from grass

## Nests

Most birds build nests in which they lay eggs. Young ones that hatch from these eggs depend on their parents for food and protection.

**Tail feathers** can be fanned out to act as a brake during landing

# Ratites

The world's largest birds are all members of a group called the ratites. All ratites are flightless. The larger species are far too heavy to fly and they, like the smaller kiwis, have a ground-based, running lifestyle.

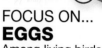

FOCUS ON...
## EGGS
Among living birds, the ratites lay the biggest eggs.

## Ostrich
*Struthio camelus*

This ratite is the world's largest bird. It is unique among birds in having only two toes on each foot. Ostriches can run at speeds of up to 45 mph (70 kph) for as long as 30 minutes.

*Black and white plumage in males*

**SIZE**  7–9 ft (2.1–2.8 m) tall

**DIET**  Mainly grass, seeds, and other plants

**HABITAT**  Savanna and semi-deserts

**DISTRIBUTION**  Western to eastern Africa (south of Sahara) and southern Africa

## Southern cassowary
*Casuarius casuarius*

This ratite plays an important role in maintaining the diversity of rainforest trees by dispersing big fruit seeds over large areas. A horny casque (crest) on top of the bird's head and wattles (fleshy growths) on its neck are unique to this bird. Females are larger than males and have a brighter neck.

**SIZE**  4¼–5½ ft (1.3–1.7 m) tall

**DIET**  Fruits

**HABITAT**  Rainforests

**DISTRIBUTION**  New Guinea and northeastern Australia

▲ Ostrich eggs are the largest in the world and can weigh more than 3 lb (1.5 kg).

▲ Kiwis lay eggs that are up to 25 percent of the body weight of the female.

▲ Several female ratites often lay in the same nest, brooded by a single male. This nest is a rhea's.

# Emu
*Dromaius novaehollandiae*

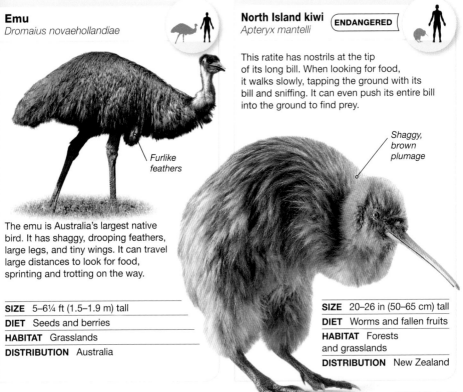

Furlike feathers

The emu is Australia's largest native bird. It has shaggy, drooping feathers, large legs, and tiny wings. It can travel large distances to look for food, sprinting and trotting on the way.

**SIZE**  5–6¼ ft (1.5–1.9 m) tall

**DIET**  Seeds and berries

**HABITAT**  Grasslands

**DISTRIBUTION**  Australia

# North Island kiwi  [ENDANGERED]
*Apteryx mantelli*

This ratite has nostrils at the tip of its long bill. When looking for food, it walks slowly, tapping the ground with its bill and sniffing. It can even push its entire bill into the ground to find prey.

Shaggy, brown plumage

**SIZE**  20–26 in (50–65 cm) tall

**DIET**  Worms and fallen fruits

**HABITAT**  Forests and grasslands

**DISTRIBUTION**  New Zealand

# Gamebirds and waterfowl

Gamebirds are mainly ground-dwelling birds. They can take to the air to escape but cannot fly for long. Waterfowl (ducks, geese, and swans) are strong swimmers with waterproof feathers and webbed feet. They are powerful fliers; many migrate great distances to breed.

## Indian peafowl
*Pavo cristatus*

The Indian peafowl is a stunning gamebird. Known as the peacock, the male peafowl shows off a magnificent fan of feathers to impress his mate. These plumes emerge from just above his short tail, hidden beneath.

**SIZE** Female 2½ ft (0.8 m) long, Male 8¼ ft (2.5 m) long

**DIET** Seeds, fruits, insects, small mammals, and reptiles

**HABITAT** Deciduous forests and farmlands

**DISTRIBUTION** India and Sri Lanka

Tail drags along ground behind the male when not fanned out

Peacocks have the longest feathers of all birds. They can be up to 6½ ft (2 m) long.

## Vulturine guineafowl
*Acryllium vulturinum*

This bird is the largest guineafowl and usually lives in large groups. It is named after its bare head and scrawny neck, which give it a vulturelike look.

**SIZE**  24–28 in (61–71 cm) long

**DIET**  Mainly plants

**HABITAT**  Mainly savanna

**DISTRIBUTION**  East Africa

## Lesser prairie chicken
*Tympanuchus pallidicinctus*

A smaller version of the greater prairie chicken, this bird was once found in prairie grassland all over North America. Farming on native prairie land has, however, restricted its habitat.

**SIZE**  15–16 in (38–41 cm) long

**DIET**  Seeds, insects, and acorns

**HABITAT**  Prairie and mixed grasslands

**DISTRIBUTION**  Southern North America

## Black swan
*Cygnus atratus*

Black swans have the longest necks of all swans. They are highly social and often flock together on lakes, but only occasionally nest together.

**SIZE**  3½–4½ ft (1.1–1.4 m) long

**DIET**  Water plants

**HABITAT**  Large, shallow lakes

**DISTRIBUTION**  Australia; introduced to New Zealand

## Mandarin duck
*Aix galericulata*

Of all the ducks, the Mandarin duck is most likely to roost and nest in holes in trees. The breeding plumage of males (below) is among the most ornate of all birds.

**SIZE**  16–20 in (41–51 cm) long

**DIET**  Plants, seeds, nuts, and insects

**HABITAT**  Trees near lakes, pools, and rivers

**DISTRIBUTION**  Northeastern Asia; introduced to western Europe

# Penguins, albatrosses, and divers

Penguins and albatrosses are seabirds. The flightless penguins live in the cold climates of the southern hemisphere, while the long-winged albatrosses are found worldwide. The divers are mainly coastal, but frequent warmer climates in winter.

## King penguin
*Aptenodytes patagonicus*

Penguins are specialized seabirds that "fly" under water by flapping their flipperlike wings. King penguins can dive to depths of up to 1,000 ft (300 m). Penguins can adjust their vision under water, which lets them catch their prey easily.

**SIZE** 37–40 in (94–100 cm) tall

**DIET** Mostly lantern fish

**HABITAT** Nests on islands, on flat beaches with no snow or ice

**DISTRIBUTION** Southern Atlantic and southern Indian oceans

## Red-throated diver
*Gavia stellata*

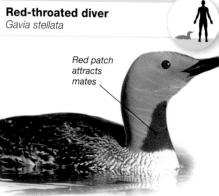

Red patch attracts mates

This diver is the smallest and lightest diver of all. When it is breeding in summer, it develops a striking throat patch that has inspired its name. The bird forms a life-long bond with its mate.

**SIZE** 21–27 in (53–69 cm) long

**DIET** Mainly fish and crustaceans

**HABITAT** Coastal bays and inlets, temperate forests, Arctic tundra, and freshwater areas

**DISTRIBUTION** Northern North America, northern Eurasia, Mediterranean Sea, Black Sea, and eastern Asia

## Black-browed albatross
*Thalassarche melanophrys*

( ENDANGERED )

Albatrosses spend most of their lives at sea, only returning to land to breed. They spend weeks at sea, gliding low over the water while hunting for fish. Once found widely, their numbers have dropped because they are victims of fishing by humans. These birds tend to catch fish with hooks still attached, often leading to their death.

*Long wing allows efficient long-distance flight*

**SIZE** 32–37½ in (80–95 cm) long

**DIET** Fish, squid, and crustaceans

**HABITAT** Open oceans and rocky areas on islands

**DISTRIBUTION** Southern oceans

## Buller's shearwater
*Puffinus bulleri*

Buller's shearwaters breed only in New Zealand, on the Poor Knights Islands.

Shearwaters are the smaller cousins of the albatrosses. The Buller's shearwater breeds on few islands and because of this limited range, it may be at risk when breeding due to disease and introduced predators. If rats or cats reach these islands, they will wipe out the species by eating eggs and chicks.

**SIZE** 18–18½ in (45–47 cm) long

**DIET** Krill, small fish, salps, and jellyfish

**HABITAT** Open oceans and islands

**DISTRIBUTION** Pacific Ocean

# Flamingos and grebes

Flamingos are tall wading birds that use their bills to sieve tiny organisms from the water. They are known to gather in flocks of up to a million birds. Grebes are superb swimmers with small heads and thin necks that help them dive easily. Both flamingos and grebes are known for their amazing courtship rituals.

## Western grebe
*Aechmophorus occidentalis*

The western grebe is the largest grebe in North America. In a dramatic courtship display, a pair rushes across the water side by side, with their long necks extended. The crown of this grebe stays black all year round.

| | |
|---|---|
| **SIZE** | 21½–29½ in (55–75 cm) long |
| **DIET** | Carp, herring, insects, and crabs |
| **HABITAT** | Marshes, lakes, and bays |
| **DISTRIBUTION** | Canada to Mexico |

## Great crested grebe
*Podiceps cristatus*

Black crest raised during courtship

Great crested grebes offer one another gifts of weed in an elaborate mating dance. They are also attentive parents. Parents take turns carrying the chicks on their backs and bringing them food.

| | |
|---|---|
| **SIZE** | 18–20 in (46–51 cm) long |
| **DIET** | Fish |
| **HABITAT** | Large, open freshwater lakes |
| **DISTRIBUTION** | Europe, Asia, Africa, Australia, and New Zealand |

# Caribbean flamingo
*Phoenicopterus ruber ruber*

The Caribbean flamingo has the brightest feathers of all flamingos. Chicks have gray plumage. Pairs of flamingos build nests of mud. A flamingo's territory is determined simply by how far its neck stretches from its nest.

**SIZE**  4–4½ ft (1.2–1.4 m) tall

**DIET**  Mainly brine shrimp

**HABITAT**  Lagoons, mudflats, and lakes

**DISTRIBUTION**  Northern coasts of South America and Mexico, Bahamas, Cuba, Dominican Republic, Haiti, Turks and Caicos Islands, and Galápagos Islands

Flamingos eat tiny shrimp that dye their feathers pink.

# Storks and herons

These birds use their long legs to wade slowly in shallow water, where they find most of their food. Long legs help keep their feathers dry. They use keen eyesight to spot prey in the water. All of them have long bills that grab prey easily.

## Roseate spoonbill
*Ajaia ajaja*

Spoonbills feed by swinging their flat, touch-sensitive bills back and forth in the water. The bare patch of skin on the roseate spoonbill's head and face turns yellow in the breeding season.

*Bright pink bar on wing*

| | |
|---|---|
| **SIZE** | 28–34 in (71–86 cm) tall |
| **DIET** | Insects and small fish |
| **HABITAT** | Shallow coastal waters |
| **DISTRIBUTION** | South America |

## Scarlet ibis
*Eudocimus ruber*

The scarlet ibis builds its nest on islands, where its eggs and young are safe from predators. Nests are usually built in trees, far above the water the birds hunt in.

| | |
|---|---|
| **SIZE** | 22–24 in (56–61 cm) long |
| **DIET** | Crustaceans, amphibians, and fish |
| **HABITAT** | Wetlands, such as estuaries |
| **DISTRIBUTION** | Tropical America |

*Black wing tip*

## American bittern
*Botaurus lentiginosus*

Striped plumage makes this heron difficult to spot in its reed home. When alarmed, it raises its head and freezes, making it even more difficult to find. Its booming mating call, however, gives the bird away.

**SIZE** 23½–29½ in (60–75 cm) tall

**DIET** Amphibians, fish, snakes, and insects

**HABITAT** Freshwater wetlands and bogs

**DISTRIBUTION** North and Central America and the Caribbean

## Marabou stork
*Leptoptilos crumeniferus*

The marabou stork is an adept scavenger. Its bare head and neck allow it to stick its head inside carcasses without soiling its feathers. It has a wide wingspan of 10 ft (3 m) that helps it to soar gracefully.

**SIZE** 4–5 ft (1.2–1.5 m) tall

**DIET** Carrion

**HABITAT** Open dry savanna and grasslands

**DISTRIBUTION** Africa

## Jabiru stork
*Jabiru mycteria*

The jabiru is the tallest flying bird in South America. It has a characteristic slightly upturned bill. These birds build large nests that they return to and add to each year. Nests may reach several metres in diameter.

**SIZE** 4–4½ ft (1.2–1.4 m) tall

**DIET** Small water animals

**HABITAT** Freshwater wetlands

**DISTRIBUTION** South America

## African openbill
*Anastomus lamelligerus*

This bird is often spotted looking for snails. Its curved bill has a distinct gap that holds the snails. It cracks open the shells and eats what is inside.

**SIZE** 32–37 in (81–94 cm) long

**DIET** Large water snails

**HABITAT** Mainly wetlands

**DISTRIBUTION** Africa and Madagascar

# Pelicans and gannets

Most members of this varied group of waterbirds are ocean-going hunters of fish. They are strong swimmers and the only group of birds with webbing between all four toes. Most pelicans fish from the surface, while gannets dive from great heights to catch shoaling fish.

## Blue-footed booby
*Sula nebouxii*

These birds, like other members of the gannet family, form strong, life-long bonds. Courtship displays are often repeated and the most impressive is the "sky-pointing ritual"—the birds flaunt their blue feet and point their beaks upward.

**SIZE** 32 in (81 cm) long

**DIET** Mainly fish

**HABITAT** Nests on rocky coasts and hunts in open oceans

**DISTRIBUTION** California to Peru and the Galápagos Islands

## Great frigatebird
*Fregata minor*

This member of the pelican family soars high up in the sky and rarely touches the ground. It has tiny legs and feet and can barely walk on land. A fierce competitor, it often attacks other birds, forcing them to give up food.

**SIZE** 33½–41 in (85–105 cm) long

**DIET** Fish and squid

**HABITAT** Nests on isolated, well-vegetated islands; open oceans

**DISTRIBUTION** South Atlantic

*Male inflates his pouch to attract mates*

## Brown pelican
*Pelecanus occidentalis*

This is the only pelican that plunges, or dives, for food. It soars as high as 33 ft (10 m) before darting into the sea to catch fish. Unlike other pelicans, it lives in coastal waters and never flies far out to sea.

**SIZE** 3¼–4½ ft (1–1.4 m) long

**DIET** Fish

**HABITAT** Coastal areas, such as sandy beaches

**DISTRIBUTION** North and South America

## Hamerkop
*Scopus umbretta*

The hamerkop is a relative of pelicans but not a seabird. Very industrious birds, males and females together build huge nests, which have a hidden entrance at the side.

**SIZE** 22 in (56 cm) long

**DIET** Mainly amphibians

**HABITAT** Forests to semi-deserts with water

**DISTRIBUTION** Africa, Madagascar, and the Arabian Peninsula

# Raptors and owls

Raptors are birds of prey with sharp eyesight and muscular legs. Many are agile fliers. These day-flying hunters have sharp beaks and talons, which kill prey. Although not related to raptors, owls have similar features, but hunt mostly at night.

## FOCUS ON... **CONTRASTS**

Raptors and owls may seem similar but there are key differences.

▲ Most raptors' eyes are on the side of the head. They can spot prey from a long way off.

▲ Owls have large, forward-facing eyes, which help them to judge distance to prey.

### Great gray owl
*Strix nebulosa*

Amazingly, the great gray owl can hear movement at a depth of 2 ft (60 cm) under snow. It usually glides to a great height before swooping in and breaking through snow-covered ground to find prey. It can prey on birds as big as a grouse.

*Disk-shaped face acts as an external ear, collecting sound and funneling it toward its ear openings*

**SIZE** 26–28 in (65–70 cm) long

**DIET** Large rodents and birds

**HABITAT** Coniferous forests

**DISTRIBUTION** Northern North America and northern Eurasia

## Andean condor
*Vultur gryphus*

This raptor has the largest wings of any bird. Its broad wings can span 10 ft (3 m) or more, and it uses them to catch rising warm air currents. It can soar in the air for hours, looking for remains of dead animals.

**SIZE**  3¼–4½ ft (1–1.4 m) long

**DIET**  Mainly carrion

**HABITAT**  Mountains

**DISTRIBUTION**  South America

## Peregrine falcon
*Falco peregrinus*

This falcon is the world's fastest bird. Peregrines spot prey from high up in the sky and swoop down at speeds of up to 200 mph (325 kph). Females are larger than males and can catch larger prey.

**SIZE**  13½–23 in (34–58 cm) long

**DIET**  Mainly birds

**HABITAT**  Nests on rock ledges

**DISTRIBUTION** Worldwide, except Antarctica

## Bald eagle
*Haliaeetus leucocephalus*

The bald eagle is the national bird of the United States. This raptor uses its clawed feet to snatch fish from near the water's surface. It may steal food from other raptors, such as ospreys. In the winter, bald eagles gather in large groups near salmon breeding sites. These birds pair for life.

**SIZE**  28–38 in (71–96 cm) long

**DIET**  Mainly fish

**HABITAT**  Near rivers, lakes, and on coasts

**DISTRIBUTION**  North America

**SNOWY OWL**
Snowy owls have thick white plumage, which helps them to hide from their prey and pounce on them with ease. They can roost undisturbed all day long in polar regions, north of the Arctic Circle—which is where these owls commonly live.

Adult snowy owls commonly eat

# five lemmings

a day, but must catch even
more when rearing chicks

# Auks, gulls, and shorebirds

These birds are a common sight at sea or near shorelines. Gulls are seabirds that use their flying skills to catch prey. Shorebirds usually feed by the water's edge. Auks generally dive under water for food. Many birds in this group nest on the ground.

## Arctic tern
*Sterna paradisaea*

The Arctic tern is a seabird that undertakes the longest migration of any animal. It journeys from the Arctic to the Antarctic and back each year. In its lifetime, an average Arctic tern travels as far as a journey to the Moon and back.

**SIZE**  13–14 in (33–35 cm) long

**DIET**  Fish and crustaceans

**HABITAT**  Tundra, lakes, and coastal lagoons

**DISTRIBUTION**  Polar regions

## Great black-backed gull
*Larus marinus*

The world's largest gull, this is a heavy and powerful bird. It is a fierce predator and even pursues big seabirds. It scavenges almost anything edible, including refuse and roadkill.

**SIZE**  25–31 in (64–78 cm) long

**DIET**  Fish, seabirds, and eggs

**HABITAT**  Mainly coasts and estuaries

**DISTRIBUTION**  North Atlantic

Pink leg and foot distinguishes gull from the lesser black-backed gull

## Ruff
*Philomachus pugnax*

This is the most spectacular looking of all waders. Males develop colorful neck collars during the breeding season, which attract females.

**SIZE** 8–12 in (20–30 cm) long

**DIET** Aquatic insects

**HABITAT** Swamps and meadows

**DISTRIBUTION** Northern Eurasia and Africa

## African jacana
*Actophilornis africanus*

The African jacana has extremely large feet that help this shorebird walk on floating plants. Males make attentive fathers and keep the chicks nestled close to keep them warm.

**SIZE** 9–12 in (23–31 cm) long

**DIET** Insects, small invertebrates, and aquatic plant seeds

**HABITAT** Wetlands

**DISTRIBUTION** West to central Africa

## Atlantic puffin
*Fratercula arctica*

Puffins belong to the auk family. Atlantic puffins have special beaks. The upper part and tongue are ridged so that they can securely hold many fish at a time. This puffin can hold its breath under water for up to 30 seconds.

**SIZE** 10–11½ in (26–29 cm)

**DIET** Small fish, such as sand eels, herring, squid, and small invertebrates

**HABITAT** Sea cliffs

**DISTRIBUTION** North Atlantic

Atlantic puffins have been known to hold as many as 62 fish in their beaks at once.

# Parrots

In the wild, these brightly colored birds gather in noisy flocks. Ranging from small budgerigars to great macaws, parrots are popular as pets and have an amazing ability to learn and mimic human sounds.

FOCUS ON...
**DIET**
Most parrots feed on plants, fruits, and nuts. Some, however, have specialized diets.

## Rosy-faced lovebird
*Agapornis roseicollis*

A small parrot found usually in dry areas, the rosy-faced lovebird often gathers at watering holes to bathe and also because it needs to drink frequently. These birds are called lovebirds because of the strong bond between a pair. Lovebirds mate for life and mutual grooming reinforces the bond between them.

| | |
|---|---|
| **SIZE** | 6½–7 in (17–18 cm) long |
| **DIET** | Leaves, seeds, and fruits |
| **HABITAT** | Woodlands and scrubby hillsides |
| **DISTRIBUTION** | Southwest Africa |

## Sulfur-crested cockatoo
*Cacatua galerita*

The bright yellow crest of the sulfur-crested cockatoos is raised when threatened or while mating. They live up to 40 years in the wild, and up to 70 years in captivity. Like many parrots, they eat clay to digest poison in some of their food.

| | |
|---|---|
| **SIZE** | 19½ in (49 cm) long |
| **DIET** | Berries, seeds, nuts, and buds |
| **HABITAT** | Forests, woodlands, and farmlands |
| **DISTRIBUTION** | New Guinea and Australia |

▲ Keas are flexible feeders. They feed on animal carcasses and leftover meat.

▲ The rainbow lorikeet collects nectar and pollen with the brushlike tip of its tongue.

▶ Budgerigars eat seeds. To remove the husks, the bird rolls each seed in its beak with its tongue.

## Blue-and-yellow macaw
*Ara ararauna*

With their colorful feathers, the blue-and-yellow macaws stand out in the rainforest canopy. They are dependent on palm trees for nesting but move around when looking for food.

*Beak is strong enough to crack brazil nuts or sever human fingers*

**SIZE** 33½ in (85 cm) long

**DIET** Fruits, flowers, and nuts

**HABITAT** Mainly nests in palm trees

**DISTRIBUTION** Northern South America

## Red fan parrot
*Deroptyus accipitrinus*

At rest, the red fan parrot's head pattern does not stand out. When alarmed, it raises its elongated neck and nape feathers, creating a rufflike effect. These fan across its head, adding to the raptorlike shape of the bird. This is the reason why this bird is also called the hawk-headed parrot.

**SIZE** 14 in (36 cm) long

**DIET** Seeds, nuts, fruits, and berries

**HABITAT** Tropical forests

**DISTRIBUTION** South America

# Hummingbirds and swifts

These birds have unique wings that make them skilled fliers. Swifts can stay aloft for years, landing only to breed. Hummingbirds can hover or even fly backward.

## FOCUS ON...
### BEAKS

Hummingbirds have long beaks that they use to suck nectar from flowers.

▲ The down-curved beak of a white-tipped sicklebill helps it probe *Heliconia* flowers for nectar.

▲ The beak of the sword-billed hummingbird helps it feed from downward-pointing flowers.

▲ The green-fronted lancebill feeds from plants using its long, almost up-curved beak.

### Common swift
*Apus apus*

The common swift has narrow wings and a forked tail. Like other swifts, it is fast and agile. It catches insects in midair in its gaping bill.

One of the most aerial birds, the common swift feeds, mates, and even sleeps in flight.

| | |
|---|---|
| **SIZE** | 6½ in (16–17 cm) long |
| **DIET** | Insects |
| **HABITAT** | Cliffs and urban areas |
| **DISTRIBUTION** | Western Europe to central Asia |

## Ruby topaz
*Chrysolampis mosquitus*

The dazzling ruby topaz is a great
traveler. Experts have not yet mapped out
all of its migration routes, but one population
is known to travel from northernmost to
southernmost Brazil. It aggressively guards
feeding territories containing its favorite
flowers. During courtship, the male circles
the female with his tail spread out like a fan.

**SIZE**   3½ in (9 cm) long

**DIET**   Nectar and insects

**HABITAT**   Forest edges
and farmlands

**DISTRIBUTION**   South America

## Lucifer hummingbird
*Calothorax lucifer*

The Lucifer hummingbird is a tiny
bird with a large head. Its long, down-curved
beak makes it easy to identify. While females
have a pale throat, males have a bright purple
throat patch.

**SIZE**   3½ in (9 cm) long

**DIET**   Mainly nectar

**HABITAT**   Semi-deserts

**DISTRIBUTION**   Southern US to Mexico

*Tiny legs and feet give hummingbirds
and swifts their group name Apodiformes,
meaning "lacking feet"*

# Woodpeckers and relatives

All birds in this group have strong feet—with two toes pointing forward and two backward—that help them climb with ease. Woodpeckers use their chisel-like beaks to carve nest holes; toucans use their long beaks for reaching fruit; and barbets use their stout beaks for holding wriggling prey.

## Greater spotted woodpecker
*Dendrocopos major*

The loud "drum-roll" of this bird is a common sound in spring. The drumming may be the sound of the bird drilling into tree bark to catch bark-boring beetle larvae, or chiseling out its nest. In spring, they use the sound to defend territories.

**SIZE** 9 in (23 cm) long

**DIET** Insects, seeds, fruits, eggs, and chicks

**HABITAT** Forests and gardens

**DISTRIBUTION** Europe to southeast Asia and North Africa

## Pileated woodpecker
*Dryocopus pileatus*

The pileated woodpecker can be recognized instantly by its spectacular red crest. It is the largest woodpecker in North America. Even though this bird lives in the same area every year, it chisels out a new nest hole each season.

**SIZE** 16–19½ in (40–49 cm) long

**DIET** Mainly ants and beetle larvae, and also fruits and nuts

**HABITAT** Forests, gardens, and wetlands

**DISTRIBUTION** North America and Mexico

## Toco toucan
*Ramphastos toco*

The largest of all toucans, this bird has an enormous beak that looks heavy but is actually very light because it is hollow. After picking up food, it tosses its head backward to move the food into its throat.

**SIZE**  21½–26 in (55–65 cm) long

**DIET**  Mainly fruits

**HABITAT**  Riverbanks, forest edges, and grasslands with plantations

**DISTRIBUTION**  Northern South America

## Chestnut-eared aracari
*Pteroglossus castanotis*

This bird is more lightly built than other toucans. Very acrobatic, it can feed on fruit even when hanging upside down.

**SIZE**  14½ in (37 cm) long

**DIET**  Mainly fruits

**HABITAT**  Forests, wetlands, and savanna

**DISTRIBUTION**  Northwestern South America

## Coppersmith barbet
*Megalaima haemacephala*

A persistent singer, the coppersmith barbet's song is a series of "tonk-tonk" notes. To attract a mate, this bird flicks its tail and puffs out its throat feathers.

**SIZE**  6½ in (17 cm) long

**DIET**  Mainly fruits

**HABITAT**  Forest edges and scrublands

**DISTRIBUTION**  Southern Asia

# Kingfishers and relatives

The birds in this group—which inctludes kingfishers, todies, bee-eaters, motmots, rollers, and hornbills—nest in holes and are found worldwide in woodlands. All of them have strong bills.

## Hoopoe
*Upupa epops*

Hoopoes have slim, down-curved bills and spend most of the day on the ground searching for food. The hoopoe call is "hoop-hoop-hoop" and it carries far. The bird raises its crest for display.

**SIZE** 10–13 in (25–32 cm) long

**DIET** Mainly invertebrates

**HABITAT** Open woodlands and grasslands

**DISTRIBUTION** Africa, Europe, and Asia

## Common kingfisher
*Alcedo atthis*

Stand by any river in Europe and you might see a common kingfisher. As soon as it spots a fish from its perch, the bird dives in vertically, folding its wings as it enters the water. A membrane protects its eyes under water.

**SIZE** 6½ in (16–17 cm) long

**DIET** Mainly fish

**HABITAT** Most aquatic habitats

**DISTRIBUTION** Europe, Asia, and northern Africa

## Red-billed hornbill
*Tockus erythrorhynchus*

One of the most common hornbills in Africa, the red-billed hornbill has a striking plumage of gray, white, and black. The male has a black patch on the lower part of its bill.

**SIZE** 16½–18 in (42–45 cm) long

**DIET** Mainly insects

**HABITAT** Savanna and open woodlands

**DISTRIBUTION** West and southwest Africa, from Senegal to Namibia

## European bee-eater
*Merops apiaster*

This colorful bird is the most widespread bee-eater. It catches insects in flight. The bird rubs the end of a bee's tail over a twig to take the venom out of its sting before eating.

**SIZE** 10–11½ in (25–29 cm) long

**DIET** Insects, mainly bees

**HABITAT** River valleys, pastures, and temperate and tropical forests

**DISTRIBUTION** Africa and southwestern Eurasia

## Lilac-breasted roller
*Coracias caudatus*

This bird sits on a high perch and looks for food below. Once it spots prey, it swoops down swiftly. It nests in a natural hole in a tree and mates for life.

**SIZE** 13–14 in (32–36 cm)

**DIET** Lizards and invertebrates, such as insects

**HABITAT** Dry woodlands

**DISTRIBUTION** South of the Sahara Desert in Africa and the southern Arabian Peninsula

## Jamaican tody
*Todus todus*

This bird's long, flat bill, with serrated edges and "whiskers" at its base is well equipped to catch insects. The bird nests in muddy banks or rotten wood.

**SIZE** 4½ in (11 cm) long

**DIET** Insects and insect larvae

**HABITAT** Mainly forests

**DISTRIBUTION** Jamaica

# Songbirds

Most of the world's birds make up a group called the passerines. Many passerines can produce complex sounds, or songs, using an organ in the throat called a syrinx. These birds are called songbirds. Males sing songs to mark their territory or to attract females.

## Blue jay
*Cyanocitta cristata*

Blue jays are often found in pairs or small groups. These birds are generally noisy, with a distinctive "peeah peeah" call. They build an open cup nest made of mud and lay up to seven eggs.

| | |
|---|---|
| **SIZE** | 10–12 in (25–30 cm) long |
| **DIET** | Acorns, other nuts and seeds, and fruits |
| **HABITAT** | Woods, parks, and gardens |
| **DISTRIBUTION** | North America |

## Superb lyrebird
*Menura novaehollandiae*

The superb lyrebird imitates not only other birds' songs but also sounds it hears in the forest, such as chainsaws and even camera clicks!

| | |
|---|---|
| **SIZE** | 32–38 in (80–96 cm) long |
| **DIET** | Ground insects |
| **HABITAT** | Rainforest |
| **DISTRIBUTION** | Southeastern Australia and Tasmania |

## Gouldian finch     ENDANGERED
*Erythrura gouldiae*

Once abundant, the Gouldian finch is now greatly reduced in number. This is because they are captured for the pet industry and have reduced food sources caused by competition with other species, and also due to habitat destruction caused by grazing.

| | |
|---|---|
| **SIZE** | 5½ in (14 cm) long |
| **DIET** | Grass seeds |
| **HABITAT** | Grassy plains |
| **DISTRIBUTION** | Northern Australia |

# Lesser bird of paradise
*Paradisaea minor*

The long feathers of a male lesser bird of paradise grow from its sides and not the wings. The bird displays them during mating. It raises its wings and shakes them to attract females. The females are, however, not brightly colored.

| | |
|---|---|
| **SIZE** | 13 in (32 cm) long |
| **DIET** | Mainly fruits |
| **HABITAT** | Island forests |
| **DISTRIBUTION** | Northern and western New Guinea |

Several males gather at "lekking grounds" to dance and impress the females. The female chooses her mate after watching the displays.

# Reptiles

Reptiles were the first vertebrates to live completely on land. Their skin is covered in waterproof scales. They form a layer that keeps moisture inside, helping reptiles to survive in hot, dry places. Most reptiles, including those that live mainly in water, lay eggs on land. The young hatch fully formed without a larval stage.

**YOUNG ONES**
Crocodile eggs have tough shells. The babies have an egg tooth, which cuts through the shell. Their mother may also lend a hand.

# Reptiles

Reptiles are cold-blooded, egg-laying vertebrates. All reptiles have scales, which may differ in shape and size. To get rid of old, worn-out scales, many reptiles shed their outer layer of skin from time to time. This process is called molting.

**Young leopard tortoise crawling out**

## Birth

Reptiles lay eggs that often have a leathery shell, which allows water and oxygen to pass through to the developing animal inside. The shell protects the egg from drying out when laid out of water.

## Types of reptile

There are four major groups of reptile—lizards and snakes; turtles and tortoises; crocodilians; and tuataras.

**Shell** is formed of many bones fused together and covered by hard plates called scutes

**Lizards and snakes** have long bodies and scaly skin. They are found in all kinds of habitat—from deserts to mountains.

**Turtles and tortoises** have bony shells, stout limbs, and a toothless, beaklike mouth. They have changed little in the last 200 million years.

**Tuataras** have wedge-shaped teeth that set them apart from lizards. The closest relatives of tuataras became extinct 100 million years ago.

**Crocodilians** are large reptiles that spend most of their time in water. They have powerful jaws that make them fierce predators.

**Reptiles are called** cold-blooded, but it does not mean that their blood is chilly. It means their body temperature changes according to their surroundings. Many reptiles control their body temperature, however, by changing their surroundings. Agamas, for instance, bask in the Sun to warm up.

Chameleons have fused, **conelike eyelids** with a small opening for the pupil

## Senses

Some reptiles rely on a combination of senses, while others, including chameleons, use one well-developed sense (sight, hearing, or smell). Chameleons can look in two different directions at the same time. They can use one eye to hunt for flying insects and the other to look out for attackers.

# Turtles and tortoises

This group of reptile has existed for about 200 million years, but is relatively unchanged in all that time. Turtles and tortoises have a hard shell that protects the soft body parts and sharp jaws used for cutting food. Turtles live in oceans or fresh water, while tortoises live mostly on land.

### Alligator snapping turtle
*Macrochelys temminckii*

The alligator snapping turtle is the world's largest freshwater turtle. It has a remarkable growth on the floor of its mouth that looks like a pink worm. Passing fish are attracted to what looks like a tasty meal, only to find the turtle's deadly jaws snapping shut. This turtle spends most of its time in the very sluggish flowing water of oxbow lakes and bayous.

**SIZE**   32 in (80 cm) long

**DIET**   Fish

**HABITAT**   Deep waters of large rivers, canals, lakes, and swamps

**DISTRIBUTION**   Southeastern United States

## Loggerhead turtle
*Caretta caretta*

ENDANGERED

This sea turtle has very powerful jaws that can easily crush crabs and lobsters. It breeds every two years but is becoming increasingly rare, as it is often a bycatch during shrimp fishing, and gets trapped in nets and drowns.

**SIZE**   4 ft (1.2 m) long

**DIET**   Hard-bodied animals, such as crabs and lobsters

**HABITAT**   Open oceans, coastal areas, and reefs

**DISTRIBUTION**   Worldwide; most common in the Mediterranean Sea and the western North Atlantic Ocean

---

## Indian starred tortoise
*Geochelone elegans*

The scutes on its knobby, high-domed shell help protect this tortoise. It is most active during the wet monsoon season.

**SIZE**   15 in (38 cm) long

**DIET**   Plants

**HABITAT**   Deserts and dry scrublands

**DISTRIBUTION**   India and Sri Lanka

---

## Pig-nosed turtle
*Carettochelys insculpta*

This turtle lacks hard scutes on its body. Pig-nosed turtles use their unique snouts to breathe air while submerged in water. They swim with flipperlike limbs bearing claws.

**SIZE**   28 in (70 cm) long

**DIET**   Snails, small fish, and fruits

**HABITAT**   Rivers, streams, lagoons, and estuaries, with water up to 23 ft (7 m) deep

**DISTRIBUTION**   New Guinea and northern Australia

# Crocodilians

Meet the giants of the reptile world. Crocodiles, alligators, caimans, and gharials form this group of formidable predators that have powerful jaws and muscular tails. Most of them live in freshwater habitats.

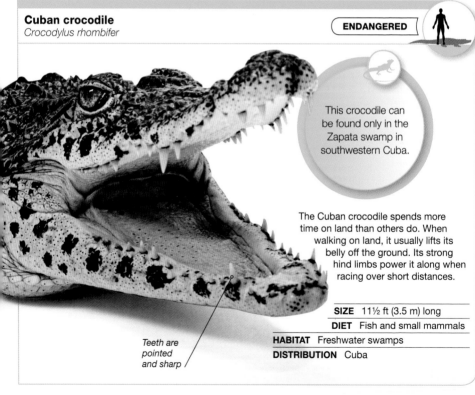

**Cuban crocodile**
*Crocodylus rhombifer*

ENDANGERED

This crocodile can be found only in the Zapata swamp in southwestern Cuba.

The Cuban crocodile spends more time on land than others do. When walking on land, it usually lifts its belly off the ground. Its strong hind limbs power it along when racing over short distances.

Teeth are pointed and sharp

| | |
|---|---|
| **SIZE** | 11½ ft (3.5 m) long |
| **DIET** | Fish and small mammals |
| **HABITAT** | Freshwater swamps |
| **DISTRIBUTION** | Cuba |

## American alligator
*Alligator mississippiensis*

Unlike other crocodilians, the American alligator can survive in freezing conditions. It keeps its nostrils above the water surface and drops its body down to warmer water below. In warmer weather, the alligator floats partly submerged in water.

**SIZE**  16½ ft (5 m) long
**DIET**  Birds, small mammals, and turtles
**HABITAT**  Lakes, swamps, and marshes
**DISTRIBUTION**  Southeastern United States

## Spectacled caiman
*Caiman crocodilus*

This caiman has a bony ridge between its eyes, making it seem like it is wearing glasses. It rarely leaves the water, unless driven out by drought. This individual is a youngster.

**SIZE**  8¼ ft (2.5 m) long
**DIET**  Reptiles, fish, amphibians, and birds
**HABITAT**  Most freshwater habitats
**DISTRIBUTION**  Central and South America

## Gharial
*Gavialis gangeticus*

ENDANGERED

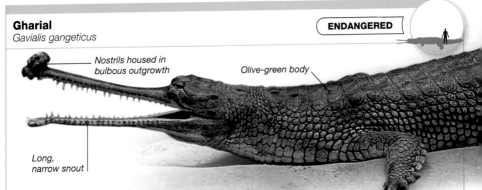

Nostrils housed in bulbous outgrowth

Olive-green body

Long, narrow snout

One of the largest members of this group, a gharial spends most of its life in water. It can barely walk on land, so it "belly slides" across the ground. Its long, thin snout has interlocking jagged teeth and is ideal for holding struggling fish.

**SIZE**  23 ft (7 m) long
**DIET**  Mainly fish, also birds or carrion
**HABITAT**  Slow-moving backwaters of rivers
**DISTRIBUTION**  Northern part of the Indian subcontinent

# Lizards

There are more species of lizard than of any other reptile. They are suited to life in arid areas and are found everywhere but Antarctica. While most lizards have four legs, some underground species are legless. Amazingly, some lizards can shed their tail to escape a predator, but grow another to replace it.

## Tokay
*Gekko gecko*

Male tokays make a loud "to-kay" call that gives this gecko its name. Like all geckos, it has sticky feet that enable it to climb easily, even on smooth surfaces. The tokay has a fierce bite.

| | |
|---|---|
| **SIZE** | 16 in (40 cm) long |
| **DIET** | Insects, small animals, and other tokays |
| **HABITAT** | Forests and buildings |
| **DISTRIBUTION** | Southeast Asia |

## Frilled lizard
*Chlamydosaurus kingii*

The large, leathery frill around the frilled lizard's neck gives this lizard its name. When it feels threatened, it opens its mouth and its umbrellalike frill, which makes it look much larger than it really is. It also rocks its body and hisses loudly. This may help to deter the predator, but if not, the lizard runs up the nearest tree.

| | |
|---|---|
| **SIZE** | 35 in (90 cm) long |
| **DIET** | Insects and other lizards |
| **HABITAT** | Subtropical woodlands |
| **DISTRIBUTION** | Australia |

## Panther chameleon
*Furcifer pardalis*

Like all chameleons, this lizard uses color to communicate—its skin changes color with its moods—and also for camouflage. Its sticky tongue is sometimes longer than its body and helps catch prey.

**SIZE** 18–22 cm (46–56 in) long

**DIET** Insects, such as crickets and mantids

**HABITAT** Deciduous tropical forests and coastal lowlands

**DISTRIBUTION** Madagascar

## Marine iguana
*Amblyrhynchus cristatus*

This is the only lizard to dive in the ocean for food. Sturdy flattened tails help marine iguanas to swim against strong currents. They have special glands in their noses that sneeze out excess salt from their seaweed diet.

**SIZE** 2¼–5 ft (0.7–1.5 m) long

**DIET** Seaweed

**HABITAT** Coasts and shallow coastal seas

**DISTRIBUTION** Galápagos Islands

## Fire skink
*Lepidothyris fernandi*

The fire skink's bright vivid colors make it a desirable pet. It is most active at twilight, when it goes foraging.

**SIZE** 14 in (35 cm) long

**DIET** Insects and spiders

**HABITAT** Forests

**DISTRIBUTION** West and central Africa

# Snakes

Long, limbless bodies and flexible jaws are the key features of these predators. Snakes can't chew so they swallow their prey whole. The upper jaw is not joined to the skull and the lower jaw opens wide and is not joined at the front, giving snakes an enormous gape.

## FOCUS ON...
## HUNTING
Snakes hunt their prey using many different techniques.

▲ Boas kill by wrapping around their victims and suffocating them.

▲ Cobras use venom to kill prey. This one sprays venom in defense.

▲ Peringuey's adders lie hidden in sand with only the black tip of their tail showing, to lure lizards.

### Green tree python
*Morelia viridis*

This long, slender tree-dwelling python drapes itself around branches, with its head hanging down, while waiting to attack prey. Its long, grasping tail helps it to climb and balance itself on tree limbs.

The scales around a python's mouth bear heat-sensitive pits that detect the body heat of warm-blooded prey.

| | |
|---|---|
| **SIZE** | 6–8 ft (1.8–2.4 m) long |
| **DIET** | Lizards and small mammals |
| **HABITAT** | Tropical forests |
| **DISTRIBUTION** | New Guinea and surrounding islands and northern Australia |

## Egyptian cobra
*Naja haje*

Mainly active at night, the Egyptian cobra is sometimes seen basking in the morning Sun. If threatened, it rears up, spreads its hood, and hisses loudly. If this doesn't work, it delivers a venomous bite, which is often fatal to humans.

**SIZE**  3¼–8 ft (1–2.4 m) long

**DIET**  Small vertebrates

**HABITAT**  Deserts and grasslands

**DISTRIBUTION**  Northwestern and East Africa

*Mouth open wide to intimidate*

## Prairie rattlesnake
*Crotalus viridis*

*Rattle*

Like all rattlesnakes, this snake warns would-be predators of its venomous bite by rattling its tail. It rattles due to a build-up of layers of old, dead scales, producing a warning "buzz." Prairie rattlesnakes hunt at night.

**SIZE**  4 ft (1.2 m) long

**DIET**  Birds, mammals, and reptiles

**HABITAT**  Grasslands, deserts, and scrublands

**DISTRIBUTION**  Midwestern United States, Mexico, and southern midwestern Canada

## Common boa
*Boa constrictor*

This snake is an ambush predator, hunting by sight and smell. It lies in wait for prey, striking out when its victim comes within reach. The boa seizes its prey in its jaws before wrapping itself around the animal and suffocating it. Small animals may be killed in seconds.

**SIZE**  Up to 13 ft (4 m) long

**DIET**  Mammals, birds, and reptiles

**HABITAT**  Open woodlands and scrublands

**DISTRIBUTION**  Central and South America

# Amphibians

The word amphibian comes from the Greek word *amphibios*, meaning "both lives." Most amphibians are adapted for life on both land and in water. Young ones have gills, which take oxygen from water. Adults of certain species retain their gills and continue living in water, while many develop air-breathing lungs for a life on land. Some land-living amphibians do not develop lungs at all, breathing through their skin instead.

**FEATHERY GILLS**
A newborn salamander breathes through its long feathery gills. When it becomes an adult, the gills shrink and it begins breathing through lungs.

# Amphibians

This group includes newts and salamanders, frogs and toads, and caecilians. There are three stages in the life of most amphibians—egg, larva, and adult. Being cold-blooded, they do not need much energy to maintain their body temperature so they may go for long periods without feeding. Their skin is moist and most species use their skin to absorb oxygen and get rid of carbon dioxide.

## Jumping

Frogs launch themselves into the air using their strong, long back legs. The front legs are bowed outward to absorb the shock of landing.

Large **thigh muscles** help to power the jump

Large, **feathery** gills

## Gills and lungs

Young amphibians breathe using external gills. Some salamanders retain these in their adult stage as well. Most frogs, toads, and salamanders on land have lungs but can also absorb some oxygen through their skin.

## Life cycle

Most amphibians start life in water, as an egg. This hatches into a larva (often called a tadpole in frogs and toads). A newt larva looks like a little fish and breathes through gills and skin. It develops lungs and changes into an adult that can also live on land.

**Newt larva hatches after two weeks**

**Egg laid by adult**

**Larva changes into adult after three to four months**

## Parenting

Most amphibians lay eggs in water. However, some species lay their eggs in damp places on land. Eggs may be laid individually or in clumps. The dusky salamander guards its eggs for 4–5 months until they hatch.

**Transparent inner eyelid** protects eye under water

**Eardrum** is on the outside of the head

## CAECILIANS

**These wormlike animals** form the smallest of the three major groups of amphibian. Caecilians lack limbs and spend their lives burrowing in moist soil.

# Salamanders and newts

These are amphibians with slender bodies and long tails. Most have four legs, but like frogs, they begin life as legless, water-dwelling larvae with a finlike tail. Only some of them leave water as adults.

## Greater siren
*Siren lacertina*

This large, long, eel-like animal spends its entire life in water. It has only one pair of legs, behind its feathery, external gills.

| | |
|---|---|
| **SIZE** | 20–35 in (50–90 cm) long |
| **DIET** | Small fish |
| **HABITAT** | Shallow water bodies |
| **DISTRIBUTION** | Southeastern United States and eastern Mexico |

## Fire salamander
*Salamandra salamandra*

The fire salamander is active mainly at night. The colorful markings on its skin warn predators that it is poisonous.

| | |
|---|---|
| **SIZE** | 7–11 in (18–28 cm) long |
| **DIET** | Worms, slugs, insects, and insect larvae |
| **HABITAT** | Forests |
| **DISTRIBUTION** | Europe |

## Great crested newt
*Triturus cristatus*

These newts normally live on land and breed in ponds. In the summer, the male develops a striking crest on its back to attract potential mates. Once the female lays an egg, she wraps it in a leaf before laying another.

| | |
|---|---|
| **SIZE** | 4–7 in (10–18 cm) long |
| **DIET** | Tadpoles, worms, insects, and their larvae |
| **HABITAT** | Ponds, lakes, and ditches |
| **DISTRIBUTION** | Europe and central Asia |

## Japanese giant salamander
*Andrias japonicus*

The Japanese giant salamander is the second largest amphibian in the world after its relative the Chinese giant salamander. Its deeply folded skin helps it to absorb oxygen from water. These salamanders hunt at night. Some have been known to live for more than 50 years.

| | |
|---|---|
| **SIZE** | 3¼–4½ ft (1–1.4 m) long |
| **DIET** | Fish, worms, and crustaceans |
| **HABITAT** | Rivers and streams |
| **DISTRIBUTION** | Japan |

*Folds of skin*

## Crocodile newt
*Tylototriton verrucosus*

This newt has a bright orange coloration that warns predators to stay away. It spends winters and dry periods underground.

*Row of poison glands*

| | |
|---|---|
| **SIZE** | 4¾–7 in (12–18 cm) long |
| **DIET** | Mainly invertebrates |
| **HABITAT** | Forests |
| **DISTRIBUTION** | Southern and Southeast Asia |

## Axolotl
*Ambystoma mexicanum* ENDANGERED

Axolotls have flat finlike tails and external gills—features that many salamanders lose as they mature. This animal retains its juvenile form throughout adulthood.

| | |
|---|---|
| **SIZE** | 4–12 in (10–30 cm) long |
| **DIET** | Mainly invertebrates, such as worms, mollusks, and insect larvae |
| **HABITAT** | Lakes |
| **DISTRIBUTION** | Mexico |

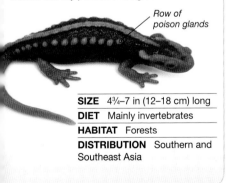

Studying the sticky feet of tree frogs may help scientists design

# self-cleaning surfaces

and long-lasting glues

**GÜNTHER'S BANDED TREE FROG**
This tree frog among forest-floor mushrooms is called Günther's banded tree frog. It is active only at night and is mostly found on trees in South America's tropical rainforests. Tree frogs form the staple diet of many types of snake.

## FOCUS ON...
# FEET
Different kinds of feet enable various frogs to live in a wide range of habitats.

▲ Tree frog toepads grip vertical surfaces due to sticky mucus and their fine, microscopic structure.

▲ Aquatic frogs' feet are webbed to form swimming paddles.

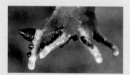

▲ The giant burrowing frog has horny "tubercles" on its hind feet, which help it to dig into soil.

# Frogs and toads

Long, powerful hind limbs and the lack of a tail set the frogs and toads apart from other amphibians. Frogs swallow prey whole, but they are not toothless—most grip prey with small teeth in their upper jaw. Some land-living frogs with warty skin are called toads.

### Cane toad
*Rhinella marinus*

This amphibian is the largest toad and also one of the most poisonous. A highly toxic juice oozes out of its shoulders if it is threatened. The clutch size of this toad is between 8,000 and 17,000.

| | |
|---|---|
| **SIZE** | 4–9½ in (10–24 cm) long |
| **DIET** | Invertebrates on land and other frogs |
| **HABITAT** | Sand dunes, mangroves, and coastal heaths |
| **DISTRIBUTION** | Central and South America; introduced to Australia |

## Orange-legged leaf frog
*Phyllomedusa hypochondrialis*

Like other tree frogs, the orange-legged leaf frog has long, slender limbs and can climb trees swiftly. It gives off an unpleasant odor to deter predators, and may even pretend to be dead to keep from being eaten.

**SIZE** 1½–2 in (4–5 cm) long

**DIET** Insects

**HABITAT** Grasslands, rainforests, and pastureland

**DISTRIBUTION** Northern to central South America

## Darwin's frog
*Rhinoderma darwinii*

This frog is named after the famous scientist Charles Darwin, who discovered it in Chile. Males are caring parents and brood their eggs by storing them inside their vocal sacs. When the eggs hatch, the tadpoles emerge from their throat.

**SIZE** ¾–1¼ in (2–3 cm) long

**DIET** Insects and other small animals

**HABITAT** Mountain forests

**DISTRIBUTION** Chile and Argentina

## Tomato frog
*Dyscophus antongilii*

The tomato frog spends the day lying buried in soil and emerges at night to hunt. It gives out a sticky secretion to protect itself from predators. This frog is also a popular pet.

**SIZE** 3¼–4¾ cm (8–12 cm) long

**DIET** Small insects and other invertebrates

**HABITAT** Rainforests

**DISTRIBUTION** Madagascar

## Asian horned frog
*Megophrys nasuta*

This horned frog lives on the forest floor. Its "horns" and folds of skin look like dry leaf edges and help the frog to hide among dead leaves while it waits for prey.

*Hornlike projection*

**SIZE** 2¾–5½ in (7–14 cm) long

**DIET** Smaller frogs, scorpions, crabs, and other invertebrates

**HABITAT** Tropical forests

**DISTRIBUTION** Southeast Asia

## Fleischmann's glass frog
*Hyalinobatrachium fleischmanni*

Glass frogs have translucent skin on the underside through which their internal organs are visible. Deforestation is shrinking the habitat of this frog.

**SIZE**  ¾–1¼ in (2–3 cm) long
**DIET**  Insects
**HABITAT**  Tropical forests and wetlands
**DISTRIBUTION**  Central and South America

## Midwife toad
*Alytes obstetricans*

This toad has a very unusual breeding style. The female lays strings of large, yolk-filled eggs and transfers them to the male's back. The male then looks after the eggs until they hatch.

**SIZE**  1¼–2 in (3–5 cm) long
**DIET**  Spiders, beetles, crickets, caterpillars, and snails
**HABITAT**  Woodlands and gardens
**DISTRIBUTION**  Western and central Europe

## Strawberry poison-dart frog
*Oophaga pumilio*

The strawberry poison-dart frog has several color variations—from brilliant blue or red to dull brown. Females carry the tadpoles and deposit them singly in tiny ponds in bromeliads (plants with vase-shaped leaves). They later feed them with their unhatched eggs.

**SIZE**  ¾–1 in (2–2.5 cm) long
**DIET**  Small arthropods, mainly ants and bugs
**HABITAT**  Tropical forests
**DISTRIBUTION**  Southern Central America

## Madagascan golden mantella
*Mantella aurantiaca*

## African bullfrog
*Pyxicephalus adspersus*

During droughts, African bullfrogs can remain underground, encased in a watertight cocoon, for several years. They emerge to breed after heavy rain. Males guard both the eggs and tadpoles. They also dig channels so that the tadpoles can reach open water.

| | |
|---|---|
| **SIZE** | 3¼–9 in (8–23 cm) long |
| **DIET** | Small insects and other frogs |
| **HABITAT** | Wet and dry savanna |
| **DISTRIBUTION** | Sub-Saharan Africa |

**ENDANGERED**

This Madagascan frog's bright colors warn that it secretes toxins. This frog is active during the day, and lives in small mixed-sex groups called armies.

| | |
|---|---|
| **SIZE** | ¾–1¼ in (2–3 cm) long |
| **DIET** | Invertebrates, such as insects |
| **HABITAT** | Rainforests |
| **DISTRIBUTION** | Madagascar |

## Broad-headed rain frog
*Craugastor megacephalus*

This frog dwells in leaf litter and even lays eggs there. It hides in a burrow and sits at the entrance at night, catching prey as they pass by. Its eggs hatch directly into small frogs.

| | |
|---|---|
| **SIZE** | 1¼–2¾ in (3–7 cm) long |
| **DIET** | Small arthropods |
| **HABITAT** | Rainforests |
| **DISTRIBUTION** | Central America |

*Feet without webs*

# Fish

Fish were the first animals with backbones to appear on the Earth, at least 500 million years ago. These cold-blooded animals have organs called gills, and in most of them the gills filter oxygen from water. Most have scales and fins. Many small fish swim in schools, moving as one. They are safer in a school because it is difficult for predators to pick out a single fish.

**SHARKS AND RAYS**
Most fish are bony, but sharks and rays are completely different—their skeletons are made of springy cartilage.

# Fish

Fish are adapted for life in water—they steer through the water using streamlined fins and use gills to absorb oxygen. Their skin has glands that secrete mucus, which protects them from bacteria. Most fish have special sensory organs that detect vibrations of other animals in water.

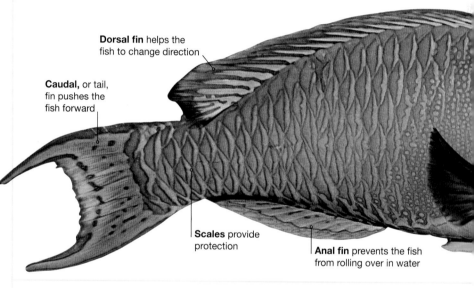

**Dorsal fin** helps the fish to change direction

**Caudal,** or tail, fin pushes the fish forward

**Scales** provide protection

**Anal fin** prevents the fish from rolling over in water

## Groups of fish

There are more than 31,000 species of fish, which fall into three groups—jawless, cartilaginous, and bony. Each of these groups had a different ancestor and evolved independently of one another.

**Jawless fish**
Unlike other vertebrates, jawless fish do not have biting jaws. Instead they have sucker disks with a rasping tongue and small teeth made of keratin.

## Living together

Some fish have highly specialized lifestyles. This bluestreak cleaner wrasse eats parasites on other fish, which often visit the wrasse's "cleaning station" for the service it provides.

**Parrotlike** beak is used to bite off fragments of coral and extract algae

**Pectoral fin** helps to change direction and can also be used for tasting and touching

## HAGFISH

Despite its name, this strange-looking animal is not actually a vertebrate. It has no backbone. It is closely related to vertebrates, though, and like them, it has a cranium, or skull.

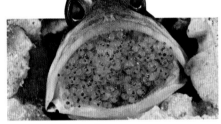

## Reproduction

Most fish produce a large number of eggs but do not provide them with any care. However, mouth brooders, such as the male jawfish, provide a safe nest for the tiny eggs in their huge mouth until the eggs hatch.

**Cartilaginous fish**
These fish have a skeleton made of cartilage instead of hard bone. Most are predators with sharp senses.

**Bony fish**
These include ray-finned fish and lobe-finned fish. They have a hard bony skeleton and a swim bladder. They swim with more precision than cartilaginous fish.

# Jawless fish and lobefins

The lampreys are the only jawless fish. They hold on to other fish with their suckerlike mouths and rasp off flesh with their teeth. The lobefinned fish form an unrelated group. They have fleshy fins that they sometimes use to "walk" on the sea- or riverbed.

## Brook lamprey
*Lampetra planeri*

These lampreys stop feeding entirely as soon as they become adults and only spawn, dying soon afterward.

Unlike most lampreys, this fish does not migrate to the sea. Adults spawn in the spring. The young are born blind and stay hidden in the riverbed for about six years, with their mouths exposed for filter feeding.

**SIZE**  6½ in (16 cm) long

**DIET**  Diatoms, algae, and dead matter

**HABITAT**  Streams, lakes, and rivers

**DISTRIBUTION**  Northern Europe and southeastern Alaska

## Coelacanth
*Latimeria chalumnae*

Coelacanths belong to a group that was thought to have died out 65 million years ago, until one was caught in 1938. Their pectoral fins are very mobile and help the fish to maneuver in tight spaces, when looking for food.

**SIZE**  6½ ft (2 m) long

**DIET**  Squid and fish

**HABITAT**  Steep, rocky underwater terrain

**DISTRIBUTION**  Seas off the Comoros Islands, Indian Ocean

*Fin has a fleshy stalk, or lobe*

## Australian lungfish
*Neoceratodus forsteri*

Unlike other lungfish, which inhabit pools that may dry up, the Australian lungfish lives in permanent bodies of water with dense vegetation. When the level of oxygen in the water falls during dry periods, it gulps air at the surface and breathes using its single lung.

**SIZE**  6 ft (1.8 m) long

**DIET**  Frogs, crabs, mollusks, and small fish

**HABITAT**  Deep pools and rivers

**DISTRIBUTION**  Eastern Australia

*Paddle-shaped, paired fins*

# Sharks and rays

Sharks are hunters with torpedo-shaped bodies, powerful jaws, sharp teeth, and a keen sense of smell. Skates and rays are cousins of sharks with broad, flat bodies. They swim by flapping their winglike fins.

**Great white shark**
*Carcharodon carcharias*

## Basking shark
*Cetorhinus maximus*

This is the world's second largest fish, after the whale shark. It feeds by swimming with its vast mouth gaping wide. Food is trapped on its gill rakers (comblike structures on its gills) as the water passes through. It often basks in the Sun at the ocean's surface.

| | |
|---|---|
| **SIZE** | 23–32¼ ft (7–9.8 m) |
| **DIET** | Plankton |
| **HABITAT** | Open oceans, diving up to 4,150 ft (1,265 m) deep |
| **DISTRIBUTION** | West and east Atlantic Ocean, Indian Ocean, and west and east Pacific Ocean |

Very large gill slits

The great white is the most feared
of all sharks. This predator strikes from
below with deadly force and can slice out a
large chunk from the body of prey in a single
bite. Its teeth are triangular and serrated.

**SIZE** 11½–20 ft (3.5–6 m)

**DIET** Seals, dolphins, and large fish

**HABITAT** Coastal waters and open oceans
up to 4,000 ft (1,220 m) deep

**DISTRIBUTION** Temperate and tropical
oceans worldwide

## Smooth hammerhead shark
*Sphyrna zygaena*

This formidable hunter moves its head
in a constant sweeping motion when hunting.
Like other sharks, it uses tiny sense organs on
its snout to detect electrical signals from prey.

**SIZE** Up
to 13 ft (4 m)

**DIET** Fish,
including rays;
crustaceans and squid

**HABITAT** Coastal waters up to
66 ft (20 m) deep

**DISTRIBUTION** Temperate and tropical
oceans worldwide

## Giant manta ray
*Manta birostris*

The biggest ray, this fish can be up to
30 ft (9 m) across. Despite its size, it can
leap out of the water when trying to avoid
large predators, such as sharks and orcas.

**SIZE** 14½–30 ft (4.5–9 m) across

**DIET** Plankton

**HABITAT** Near rocky coral reefs up to 390 ft
(120 m) deep

**DISTRIBUTION** Tropical and warm
temperate waters

## Blue-spotted ribbontail ray
*Taeniura lymma*

Blue-spotted ribbontail rays often bury
themselves in the sand on the seabed, with
only their eyes exposed, for safety. This also
camouflages them from prey as they lie in wait.

**SIZE** 28–35 in (70–90 cm) long

**DIET** Mollusks, crabs, shrimp,
and worms

**HABITAT** Sandy patches in reefs

**DISTRIBUTION**
Indian Ocean and
western
Pacific
Ocean

# Ray-finned fish

Most fish belong to this highly diverse group. They have a hard skeleton made of bone and their fins are supported by a fan of jointed rods called rays.

### Arapaima
*Arapaima gigas*

This river predator is one of the world's largest freshwater fish. It hunts large fish and even birds. Its powerful tail fins help it to lunge forward to grab prey. It breathes air through its swim bladder, which through evolution has grown and adapted to become a simple lung.

Gray to green body

The arapaima is as heavy as 3 cows—an amazing 441 lb (200 kg).

| | |
|---|---|
| **SIZE** | Up to 14¾ ft (4.5 m) long |
| **DIET** | Fish and crustaceans |
| **HABITAT** | Rivers |
| **DISTRIBUTION** | South America |

## European sturgeon
*Acipenser sturio*

ENDANGERED

This fish lives in the sea, but in the breeding season it may travel as far as 620 miles (1,000 km) up the river where it was born. The demand for caviar—made from the eggs of the sturgeon—has brought this fish to the brink of extinction.

| | |
|---|---|
| **SIZE** | Up to 11½ ft (3.5 m) long |
| **DIET** | Marine worms, shrimp, and fish |
| **HABITAT** | Coastal waters and rivers |
| **DISTRIBUTION** | Gironde River, France |

## Jewel moray eel
*Muraena lentiginosa*

Moray eels feed in a unique way. After their front teeth seize prey, a second set of jaws in their throat comes forward, grips the prey and pulls it down the throat.

*Spotted skin helps it hide*

| | |
|---|---|
| **SIZE** | 23½ in (60 cm) long |
| **DIET** | Crustaceans and fish |
| **HABITAT** | Coral reefs |
| **DISTRIBUTION** | Eastern Pacific Ocean |

## Longnose gar
*Lepisosteus osseus*

The longnose gar is a stealth hunter. It hangs motionless in the water, hidden by aquatic plants. Then with a sudden thrust, it attacks unsuspecting prey. Long jaws armed with needlelike teeth grip the struggling prey.

| | |
|---|---|
| **SIZE** | 6 ft (1.8 m) long |
| **DIET** | Mainly fish |
| **HABITAT** | Seas and wetlands |
| **DISTRIBUTION** | Central and eastern North America |

*Diamond-shaped scales*

# Sargassum fish
*Histrio histrio*

Spotted skin helps
this fish to blend in
with its surroundings

The sargassum fish can swallow prey as large as itself.

This fish is well camouflaged—it blends in with the drifting sargassum weeds in which it lives. When hunting, the sargassum fish uses a spine on its back to lure prey. Males violently nip and chase females during courtship.

**SIZE** 8 in (20 cm) long

**DIET** Mainly crustaceans and fish

**HABITAT** Floating beds of sargassum seaweed; open ocean surface waters

**DISTRIBUTION** Tropical and subtropical seas worldwide

Leglike pectoral
fin can be used
for walking on
seabed

## Atlantic herring
*Clupea harengus*

Small plankton-eating fish of the open ocean, such as this one, feed by swimming into the current with their mouths open. This herring moves to deeper waters in the day.

**SIZE**  18 in (45 cm) long

**DIET**  Plankton

**HABITAT**  Open oceans

**DISTRIBUTION**  Northeastern Atlantic Ocean, North Sea, and Baltic Sea

## Red piranha
*Pygocentrus nattereri*

Red piranhas have a fearsome reputation. They usually hunt on their own, but when hunting in groups, they can attack and kill larger animals, such as the capybara.

**SIZE**  13 in (33 cm) long

**DIET**  Fish and insects

**HABITAT**  Rivers

**DISTRIBUTION**  North, central, and eastern South America

## John Dory
*Zeus faber*

This fish has a disk-shaped body, which makes it difficult to spot from front or behind. When hunting, it can extend its jaw quickly to capture small fish.

**SIZE**  35 in (90 cm) long

**DIET**  Small fish

**HABITAT**  Coastal marine waters

**DISTRIBUTION**
Eastern Atlantic, Mediterranean Sea, Black Sea, Indian Ocean, and Pacific Ocean

## Striped eel catfish
*Plotosus lineatus*

Many catfish live in freshwater habitats, but this is the only marine species and is found on coral reefs. A very alert fish, it defends itself with a trio of poisonous spines.

**SIZE**  13 in (32 cm) long

**DIET**  Mainly invertebrates, such as oysters and sponges, and fish

**HABITAT**  Reefs, estuaries, and sea grass beds

**DISTRIBUTION**  Indian Ocean, western Pacific

**LIONFISH**
This fish hunts at night and moves to deeper water to find prey. It relies on camouflage and lightning-fast reflexes to hunt its prey—mainly fish and shrimp. It can also sweep up and trap prey with its extended pectoral fins.

The lionfish
can expand its
stomach more than

# 30 times

its original size
to take in large
amounts of food

## Turbot
*Psetta maxima*

Turbot fish have an amazing ability to alter their color to match the seabed, which helps them avoid the attention of predators most of the time. Females can lay as many as 15 million eggs.

**SIZE** 3¼ ft (1 m) long

**DIET** Fish and crustaceans

**HABITAT** Seabed

**DISTRIBUTION** Northern Atlantic, Mediterranean Sea, and Black Sea

## Weedy seadragon
*Phyllopteryx taeniolatus*

Seahorses have tough body coverings that make them stiff. This is one of the largest seahorses. It has bizarre "leaves" all over that help it hide in its seaweed home.

**SIZE** 18 in (46 cm) long

**DIET** Small invertebrates

**HABITAT** On the bed of shallow seas

**DISTRIBUTION** Waters off southern Australia

## Red lionfish
*Pterois volitans*

The spines of a red lionfish are venomous and can deliver a very painful but rarely fatal sting.

Fleshy "whiskers" help hide its large, open mouth when approaching prey

The red lionfish is a menacing hunter. It stalks prey and corners its victim by spreading out its wide fins on each side, then snapping up prey with lightning speed. It usually floats slightly head down in water, ready to pounce on prey.

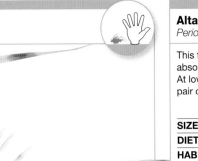

### Altantic mudskipper
*Periophthalmus barbarus*

This fish can survive out of water by absorbing oxygen from the air through its skin. At low tide, it skips over mudflats using its front pair of fins as legs.

**SIZE**   10 in (25 cm) long

**DIET**   Small animals on the mud surface

**HABITAT**   Mangroves and other tidal mudflats

**DISTRIBUTION**   Eastern Atlantic

### Clown anemonefish
*Amphiprion ocellaris*

The colorful clown anemonefish cleans algae off its host—the giant sea anemone. A special slime on its skin protects the fish from its host's sting.

**SIZE**   4½ in (11 cm) long

**DIET**   Algae and fish leftovers from sea anemone

**HABITAT**   Waters near coral reefs

**DISTRIBUTION**   Western Pacific Ocean

**SIZE**   15 in (38 cm) long

**DIET**   Fish and crustaceans

**HABITAT**   Coral and rock reefs

**DISTRIBUTION**   Pacific Ocean

# Invertebrates

Invertebrates were the first animals to evolve on the Earth. Today, they make up almost 97 percent of all animal life and range from simple animals, such as sponges, to animals with large brains and complex networks of nerves, such as squid and octopus. What they all have in common is the lack of a backbone. Other invertebrates include corals, worms, snails, starfish, and the most numerous of all, insects.

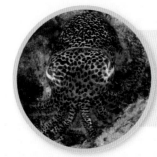

**FLASHING LIGHT**
This bobtail squid flashes light from photophores (special organs containing light-emitting bacteria) for disguise and communication.

# Invertebrates

Invertebrates make up the majority of animals on the Earth. They form many separate groups and exhibit an extraordinary variety of shapes and sizes—from corals attached to the seabed to the winged insects, which were the first kind of animal to evolve powered flight.

## Types of invertebrate

Invertebrates are highly varied and rather than forming a single natural group, they belong to many different groups. They range from simple-bodied sponges to predators such as squid.

**Sea urchins have a spherical skeleton covered by movable spines, which help them move.**

**Cuttlefish have two long tentacles that they use to catch prey.**

## Life cycle

Most invertebrates have separate larval and adult stages and often look and live entirely differently. Some look like miniature versions of their parents when they hatch, but many start life with a very different body form. They start their life as an egg, undergoing changes in shape as they grow. This process is called metamorphosis.

Once out, the caterpillar eats the egg shell

Swallowtail butterfly lays egg on a stem or a leaf.

The caterpillar bites its way through the egg shell.

# REPRODUCTION

**Some invertebrates,** including aphids in summer, can reproduce asexually. One organism gives rise to many offspring that are exact copies of it.

**Most invertebrates,** including damselflies, reproduce sexually. Females mate with males to produce offspring that inherit features from both parents.

## Living in groups

Many invertebrates live in groups called colonies, including corals and insects, such as bees and termites. Insect colonies are often devoted to a single breeding female—the queen. Most members are workers that perform different duties.

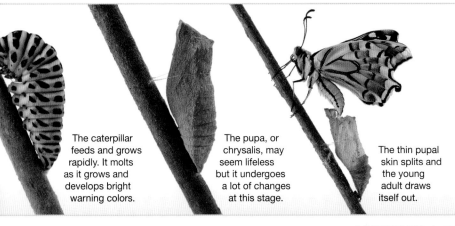

The caterpillar feeds and grows rapidly. It molts as it grows and develops bright warning colors.

The pupa, or chrysalis, may seem lifeless but it undergoes a lot of changes at this stage.

The thin pupal skin splits and the young adult draws itself out.

# Sponges, corals, and jellyfish

Sponges attach to the seabed as adults, as do corals. Their larvae are mobile, as are those of jellyfish. All of these have a single body opening and food and waste pass through it.

## Dahlia anemone
*Urticina felina*

Sea anemones look like flowers but are actually animals. The dahlia anemone has sticky swellings on the sides of its body and the sand sticks to them. This camouflages the anemone when it retracts its tentacles, making it look like a pile of gravel.

*Tentacles used to trap food*

| | |
|---|---|
| **SIZE** | 4–4¾ in (10–12 cm) long |
| **DIET** | Small fish and crustaceans |
| **HABITAT** | Shallow ocean floor |
| **DISTRIBUTION** | Arctic Ocean |

## Lobed brain coral
*Lobophyllia sp.*

Corals are made up of individual animals, called polyps, living together and forming what is known as a colony. The brain coral grows in deeper water on the sea-facing side of reefs. Each polyp of the lobed brain coral is large compared to most coral polyps—about 1¼ in (3 cm) or more in diameter.

| | |
|---|---|
| **SIZE** | 3¼–10 ft (1–3 m) long |
| **DIET** | Plankton |
| **HABITAT** | Shallow seabed |
| **DISTRIBUTION** | Indian Ocean and Pacific Ocean |

## Pink vase sponge
*Niphates digitalis*

Sponges spend their adult lives fixed to one place. They pump water in through small holes in their sides and out through the large opening at the top, filtering out tiny food particles from the current. The pink vase sponge varies in shape from a tube to an open vase.

**SIZE** 12 in (30 cm) tall

**DIET** Plankton

**HABITAT** Tropical reefs

**DISTRIBUTION**
Caribbean Sea

## Lion's mane jellyfish
*Cyanea capillata*

Most jellyfish are harmless but some, such as the lion's mane jellyfish, can deliver a painful sting. Its numerous long tentacles act like fishing lines in catching food. Its translucent, domed bell opens and closes like a big umbrella.

**SIZE** 1½–6½ ft (0.5–2 m) long

**DIET** Plankton and small fish

**HABITAT** Open oceans and coastal waters

**DISTRIBUTION** Arctic Ocean

Tentacles arranged in dense groups

# Worms

Countless types of worm live in many different habitats—in burrows, in the soil, in the sea, and as parasites inside bigger animals. The major groups of worm include the roundworms, segmented worms, and flatworms.

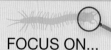
## Black and yellow flatworm
*Pseudoceros dimidiatus*

Bright colors deter predators

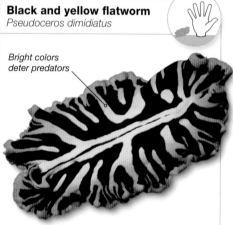

Among flatworms there are many parasites, but the sea-living black and yellow flatworm is free-living. It swims by rippling its paper-thin body, which helps it absorb oxygen from water.

| | |
|---|---|
| **SIZE** | 2¾–3 in (7–7.6 cm) long |
| **DIET** | Decaying plant and animal matter |
| **HABITAT** | Coral reefs |
| **DISTRIBUTION** | Indian Ocean and Pacific Ocean |

## Christmas tree tube worm
*Spirobranchus giganteus*

The Christmas tree tube worm is named after its extravagant whorls of tentacles, which it uses to filter food and take in oxygen. Most of its body is hidden within a tube into which it can withdraw entirely if threatened. It then covers the top of the tube with a hatch like a snail's.

▲ This ribbon worm lives on the seabed, but some live in freshwater or on land.

▲ Velvet worms have many pairs of stubby "legs" and attack insect prey by spraying it with slimy mucus.

▲ Horseshoe worms are marine animals with as many as 15,000 feeding tentacles.

**SIZE** 1½–2¾ in (4–7 cm) long

**DIET** Plankton

**HABITAT** Tropical reefs

**DISTRIBUTION** Caribbean

Individual Christmas tree tube worms may live for a decade or longer. Some live for more than 40 years.

Whorls of feeding tentacles

## Large intestinal roundworm
*Ascaris* sp.

This parasite enters the human host when the person eats food contaminated with its eggs. The larvae travel to the lungs through the blood, moving to the intestine as adults. The female produces millions of eggs, which pass out of the host in the feces.

**SIZE** 6–14 in (15–35 cm) long

**DIET** Nutrients from host's digested food; blood

**HABITAT** Host body

**DISTRIBUTION** Tropical and subtropical regions

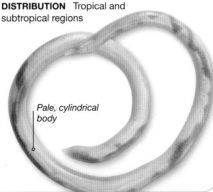

Pale, cylindrical body

# Mollusks

This group of invertebrates includes the slugs, snails, oysters, clams, octopuses, squid, and cuttlefish. Most mollusks have a soft body and a muscular base called a foot. Many have protective shells and feed using a moving ribbon of teeth called radula.

FOCUS ON...
## SHELLS
Mollusk shells contain a mineral called calcium carbonate.

**Land snail**

▲ Gastropods are mollusks with a single shell. Most use their muscular foot to crawl.

**Clam**

▲ Bivalves have a shell with two halves, or valves. Powerful muscles pull and hold the shells closed.

**Octopus**

▲ Shells of cephalopods, such as squid, are inside their body. Octopuses, however, lack shells.

### Chambered nautilus
*Nautilus pompilius*

The cephalopods form one group of mollusk and most of them lack external shells. Nautiluses are the only cephalopods that have one. The shell has gas-filled chambers that help the animal float at the right depth. The chambered nautilus has about 90 tentacles that lack suckers.

*External shell is pearly*

| | |
|---|---|
| **SIZE** | 6–9½ in (15–24 cm) long |
| **DIET** | Small fish, shrimp, and other crustaceans |
| **HABITAT** | Slopes beneath coral reefs up to 2,000 ft (600 m) deep |
| **DISTRIBUTION** | Indian Ocean and Pacific Ocean |

## Marbled chiton
*Chiton marmoratus*

Chitons are not cephalopods. They form another group of mollusks with shells made up of a series of plates. The plates are made up of a chalky mineral called aragonite.

**SIZE** 3¼ in (8 cm) long

**DIET** Algae and microbe films on rocks

**HABITAT** Rocks in coastal waters

**DISTRIBUTION** Caribbean

## Common cuttlefish
*Sepia officinalis*

This cuttlefish rests on the seabed but swims when hunting, moving by forcing a jet of water out of its body. The common cuttlefish migrates inshore to lay eggs on muddy sediments.

**SIZE** 16–20 in (40–50 cm) long

**DIET** Mollusks, shrimp, and other crustaceans

**HABITAT** Coastal waters

**DISTRIBUTION** Seas off Europe and South Africa

## Common octopus
*Octopus vulgaris*

The common octopus is one of the most intelligent invertebrates. It has excellent vision, eight muscular arms, and a horny beak. It is short-lived, however, surviving for only about two years.

*Tough skin can change color*

**SIZE** 5–10 ft (1.5–3 m) tentacle span

**DIET** Crustaceans and shelled mollusks

**HABITAT** Rocky coastal waters

**DISTRIBUTION** Tropical and warm temperate regions

## Giant African land snail
*Achatina fulica*

This is the largest land-dwelling snail.
When introduced anywhere, its numbers increase
and it becomes a pest. Like many gastropods, it
is both male and female at the same time.

| | |
|---|---|
| **SIZE** | 6–9 in (15–22 cm) long |
| **DIET** | Plants, fruits, and vegetables |
| **HABITAT** | Coastlands, forests, wetlands, and urban areas |
| **DISTRIBUTION** | East Africa |

## Giant clam
*Tridacna gigas*

The giant clam is the world's biggest bivalve. It
opens up in the day exposing its fleshy lips that
contain millions of algae. Sunlight helps the
algae make their own food by photosynthesis,
and some of this food is used by the clam. The
clam is also a filter feeder.

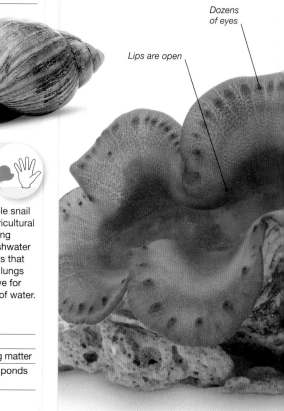

Dozens
of eyes

Lips are open

## Channeled apple snail
*Pomacea canaliculata*

The voracious appetite
of the channeled apple snail
has made it an agricultural
pest in rice-farming
areas. It is a freshwater
species with gills that
can function as lungs
so it can survive for
periods out of water.

| | |
|---|---|
| **SIZE** | 4–6 in (10–15 cm) long |
| **DIET** | Grass, animal matter, and decaying matter |
| **HABITAT** | Freshwater habitats, such as ponds and lakes |
| **DISTRIBUTION** | Tropical Americas |

**SIZE** 3¼–4½ ft (1–1.4 m) long

**DIET** Sugars made by algae and particles of food floating nearby

**HABITAT** Seabed

**DISTRIBUTION** Indian Ocean and Pacific Ocean

*Water flows through siphon, creating a current for feeding and absorbing oxygen*

The amazing color of the giant clam comes from the algae that find a safe haven in its flesh.

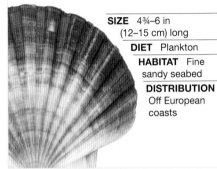

## Great scallop
*Pecten maximus*

Like all scallops, the great scallop rests on the seabed, with its shells slightly open. If disturbed, it clamps down its shells, squirting a jet of water that pushes it along.

**SIZE** 4¾–6 in (12–15 cm) long

**DIET** Plankton

**HABITAT** Fine sandy seabed

**DISTRIBUTION** Off European coasts

## Sunburst carrier shell
*Stellaria solaris*

This sea snail often cements pebbles or shells of other snails and clams on to its own for protection. Its spines help raise the shell up off the ocean floor.

**SIZE** Up to 5 in (13 cm) long

**DIET** Algae

**HABITAT** Near the seabed, up to 820 ft (250 m) deep

**DISTRIBUTION** Indian Ocean, Red Sea, and Pacific Ocean

*Spines may break when older*

# Arthropods

Four out of five animal species are arthropods. They form by far the largest group of invertebrates. They include insects, spiders, and crabs, all of which have a tough outer covering, or exoskeleton.

FOCUS ON...
**APPENDAGES**
Arthropod means "jointed legs." Arthropods have legs made of jointed units.

---

### European pill millipede
*Glomeris marginata*

Millipedes have between 36 and 450 legs, two pairs growing from each body segment. Pill millipedes are short, squat species with only 11–13 body segments. Like all pill millipedes, it rolls itself into a tight ball if attacked by a predator, such as a snail or a bird. It can look like a woodlouse, although its size and number of legs are a giveaway.

**SIZE** ½–¾ in (0.6–2 cm) long

**DIET** Decaying leaves

**HABITAT** Soil and leaf litter in broad-leaved forests

**DISTRIBUTION** Europe, parts of Asia, and northern Africa

---

### Tiger giant centipede
*Scolopendra hardwickei*

Centipede means "100 legs," but surprisingly, no species has exactly 100. The average centipede has 50 legs, but the greatest number of legs recorded for a centipede is 382. Most are active at night. They use their venomous claws to kill prey. Many giant species, such as the tiger giant centipede, have vibrant warning colors.

**SIZE** 8–10 in (20–25 cm) long

**DIET** Invertebrates and small vertebrates

**HABITAT** Under rotting wood, loose bark, and leaf litter in rainforests

**DISTRIBUTION** Southeast Asia

*One pair of jointed legs per body segment*

▲ Centipedes are arthropods with at least 16 body segments, each carrying one pair of legs.

▲ Spiders have four pairs of legs and two pairs of feeding appendages, but lack antennae.

▲ Crabs, lobsters, and shrimps have 10 legs. The first pair forms pincers.

▲ Insects, such as this beetle, have six legs, all attached to the middle body section, or thorax.

## Horseshoe crab
*Limulus polyphemus*

Despite their name, these animals are not crabs. They are most closely related to arachnids (spiders and scorpions). They get their name from the horseshoe-shaped shell, or carapace, which covers their entire body, except the tail.

**SIZE** 16–23½ in (40–60 cm) long

**DIET** Mollusks, worms, other marine animals

**HABITAT** Shallow seas

**DISTRIBUTION** Eastern coast of North America, particularly the Gulf of Mexico

## Yellow-kneed sea spider
Callipallenidae

*One of eight multicolored, jointed legs*

Sea spiders are not related to arachnids (spiders and scorpions). They have no breathing organs but can absorb oxygen through their skin.

**SIZE** 2–4 in (5–10 cm) across

**DIET** Soft-bodied marine animals, such as sponges, anemones, lace corals, and hydroids

**HABITAT** Coral reefs

**DISTRIBUTION** Coral reefs around Australia

## Vernal pool tadpole shrimp
*Lepidurus packardi*

**ENDANGERED**

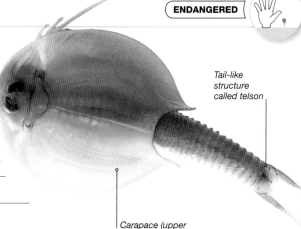

This shrimp has changed little in millions of years. It is adapted to life in vernal pools—temporary pools filled by spring rain—since its eggs can survive drying out for up to 10 years. Once hatched, the shrimp can mature in only 25 days.

Tail-like structure called telson

**SIZE**  2 in (5 cm) long

**DIET**  Fairy shrimp, insect larvae, and other invertebrates

**HABITAT**  Vernal pools and other freshwater bodies

**DISTRIBUTION**  US, mainly California

Carapace (upper section of shell)

---

## Common lobster
*Homarus gammarus*

The common lobster smells prey with its long antennae, since it hunts in darkness. It uses its larger claw to crush the hard shell of its prey and the other to cut it.

**SIZE**  Up to 2 ft (50 cm) long

**DIET**  Mollusks and crustaceans

**HABITAT** Continental shelf

**DISTRIBUTION** Eastern Atlantic Ocean

---

## White-spotted hermit crab
*Dardanus megistos*

The white-spotted hermit crab is "left-handed"—it has an enlarged left claw. Hermit crabs have softer bodies than other crabs, so they live in abandoned sea snail shells to protect themselves. These crabs are quite large and scavenge for food.

**SIZE**  5–8 in (13–20 cm) long

**DIET**  Algae, tubeworms, and fish

**HABITAT**  Sandy, rocky shores

**DISTRIBUTION**  Coasts of the eastern Atlantic Ocean, Indian Ocean, and Pacific Ocean

## Peacock mantis shrimp
*Odontodactylus scyllarus*

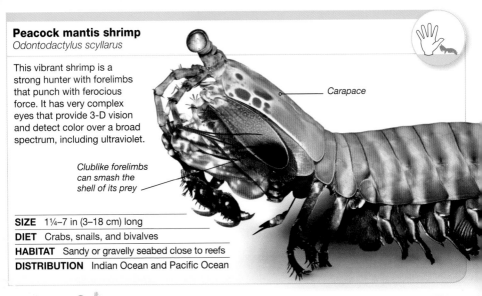

This vibrant shrimp is a strong hunter with forelimbs that punch with ferocious force. It has very complex eyes that provide 3-D vision and detect color over a broad spectrum, including ultraviolet.

Carapace

Clublike forelimbs can smash the shell of its prey

**SIZE** 1¼–7 in (3–18 cm) long

**DIET** Crabs, snails, and bivalves

**HABITAT** Sandy or gravelly seabed close to reefs

**DISTRIBUTION** Indian Ocean and Pacific Ocean

## Panamic arrow crab
*Stenorhynchus debilis*

The Panamic arrow crab is a type of spider crab. It has 10 long, spiderlike legs. It is small and stalk-eyed. The elongated front of its head gives it a triangular appearance. This scavenger is active mostly at night.

**SIZE** ½–1¼ in (1–3 cm) long

**DIET** Algae and snails

**HABITAT** Reef crevices

**DISTRIBUTION** Eastern Pacific Ocean

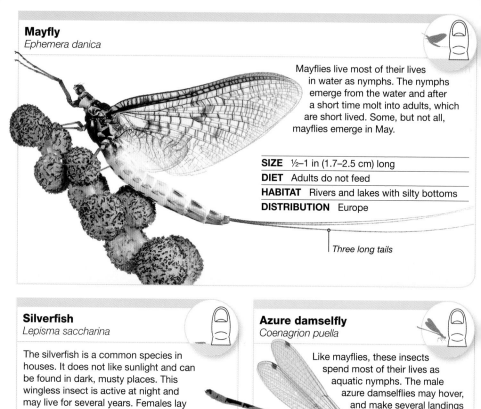

## Mayfly
*Ephemera danica*

Mayflies live most of their lives in water as nymphs. The nymphs emerge from the water and after a short time molt into adults, which are short lived. Some, but not all, mayflies emerge in May.

| | |
|---|---|
| **SIZE** | ½–1 in (1.7–2.5 cm) long |
| **DIET** | Adults do not feed |
| **HABITAT** | Rivers and lakes with silty bottoms |
| **DISTRIBUTION** | Europe |

*Three long tails*

## Silverfish
*Lepisma saccharina*

The silverfish is a common species in houses. It does not like sunlight and can be found in dark, musty places. This wingless insect is active at night and may live for several years. Females lay their eggs in small crevices.

| | |
|---|---|
| **SIZE** | ½ in (1.2 cm) long |
| **DIET** | Small insects, damp textiles, and paper |
| **HABITAT** | Tree canopies, caves, and human dwellings |
| **DISTRIBUTION** | Worldwide |

## Azure damselfly
*Coenagrion puella*

Like mayflies, these insects spend most of their lives as aquatic nymphs. The male azure damselflies may hover, and make several landings on the water, to convince the females to lay their eggs there.

| | |
|---|---|
| **SIZE** | 1½ in (3.5 cm) long |
| **DIET** | Water crustaceans (as nymphs); insects (as adults) |
| **HABITAT** | Small ponds and streams |
| **DISTRIBUTION** | Central and southern Europe to central Asia |

## Foaming grasshopper
*Dictyophorus spumans*

This grasshopper's vivid colors warn predators to stay away. If threatened, it produces a toxic chemical from glands in its thorax.

**SIZE**  2½–3¼ in (6–8 cm) long

**DIET**  Plants

**HABITAT**  Open, rocky, low vegetation

**DISTRIBUTION**  South Africa

## Oak bush cricket
*Meconema thalassinum*

A shy creature, the oak bush cricket does not really have a song like most crickets. Instead, it drums on leaves with its hind legs. This small insect comes out to feed after dark.

**SIZE**  ¾ in (1.8–2 cm) long

**DIET**  Small insects

**HABITAT**  Broad-leaved forests

**DISTRIBUTION**  Europe; introduced to US

## Jungle nymph stick insect
*Heteropteryx dilatata*

Jungle nymph stick insects hiss and splay their hind legs if attacked. Males can fly a short distance, but females do not fly because they have only stubby wings, like an immature nymph. This inspired the name of this species.

*Small, non-overlapping wing pads show that this female is still a nymph, although adults' wings are not much bigger*

**SIZE**  Up to 6¼ in (15.5 cm) long

**DIET**  Foliage of various plants

**HABITAT**  Tropical forests

**DISTRIBUTION**  Malaysia

The horse-head grasshopper
is also called the
# jumping stick
because it looks like a stick
insect but can leap like
a grasshopper

**HORSE-HEAD GRASSHOPPER**
This grasshopper lives in the tropical rainforests of Peru. It has evolved the same kind of camouflage as the stick insect. This disguise helps it avoid being seen by predators. If disturbed, it freezes.

## Javanese leaf insect
*Phyllium bioculatum*

Leaf insects' ability to mimic leaves helps them hide from predators. This species pretends to be a dead wrinkled leaf and completes the pretense by swaying in the breeze.

**SIZE** 2¾–3¾ in (7–9.4 cm) long

**DIET** Mainly leaves of fruit trees

**HABITAT** Tropical rainforests

**DISTRIBUTION** Southeast Asia

*Fake leaf veins, holes, and blotches*

## Hover fly
*Syrphus ribesii*

This insect may look like a wasp, but it is a fly. Predators keep a distance, fearing a sting. Hover flies are among the most skilled fliers. They often hover over flowers or dart after others of their kind in a high-speed chase.

**SIZE** ½ in (1.2 cm) long

**DIET** Nectar and pollen (as adults)

**HABITAT** Flower-rich meadows

**DISTRIBUTION** Europe

## Orchid mantis
*Hymenopus coronatus*

The orchid mantis lurks among white orchids, waiting quietly for its prey to come within range. It quickly grabs its victim with long, spiked forelegs.

**SIZE** 1¼–2½ in (3–6 cm) long

**DIET** Mainly insects

**HABITAT** Rainforests

**DISTRIBUTION** Southeast Asia

## Jeweled frog beetle
*Sagra buqueti*

Collectors prize the attractive jeweled frog beetle. It has strong froglike hind legs that it uses in defense or in male-to-male combat. Like all beetles, it has hard forewings called elytra, which form a protective case over the hind wings.

**SIZE** 1¼–1½ in (3–3.5 cm) long

**DIET** Leaves and pollen

**HABITAT** Most plants

**DISTRIBUTION** Southeast Asia, mainly Thailand

# Wart-headed bug
*Phrictus quinquepartitus*

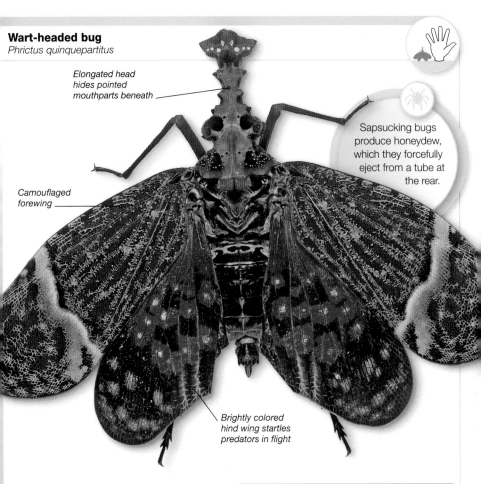

Elongated head hides pointed mouthparts beneath

Camouflaged forewing

Sapsucking bugs produce honeydew, which they forcefully eject from a tube at the rear.

Brightly colored hind wing startles predators in flight

Also known as the "dragon-headed bug," this species has a bizarrely shaped head. It belongs to a group of insects called the bugs, none of which can bite or eat solid food. Instead, it uses its pointed beak to stab plants and suck up sap.

| | |
|---|---|
| **SIZE** | 2¼ in (5.5 cm) long |
| **DIET** | Sap of plants and trees |
| **HABITAT** | Forests |
| **DISTRIBUTION** | Costa Rica, Panama, Colombia, and parts of Brazil |

## Madagascan hissing cockroach
*Gromphadorhina portentosa*

This cockroach startles predators by making a hissing noise by forcing air through its breathing holes. It is flightless, unlike other cockroaches.

**SIZE**   2–3¼ in (5–8 cm) long

**DIET**   Decaying matter and dung

**HABITAT**   Tropical forests and caves

**DISTRIBUTION**   Madagascar

## Cairns birdwing butterfly
*Ornithoptera priamus*

Birdwings are among the world's largest butterflies. The Cairns birdwing is vulnerable and protected by Australian law. Females are bigger than males but are less colorful. The caterpillars deter predators by producing a foul-smelling odor.

**SIZE**   6½–7 in (16–18 cm) wingspan

**DIET**   Nectar (as adults)

**HABITAT**   Flower-rich tropical forests

**DISTRIBUTION**   From Papua New Guinea and Solomon Islands to tropical North Australia

## American Moon moth
*Actias luna*

These delicately colored night-flying moths have heavy bodies and broad, beautifully marked wings. In adults, the mouth parts do not work. Adults have only two functions—to mate and to produce eggs.

**SIZE**   2¾–4½ in (7–11 cm) wingspan

**DIET**   Young feed on the leaves of deciduous trees; adults don't feed

**HABITAT**   Tropical and subtropical forests

**DISTRIBUTION**   North America

Long hind-wing tail

## Splendid emerald wasp
*Stilbum splendidum*

The splendid emerald wasp is a parasite of mud-nesting wasps. The female lays an egg in the nest and when her larva hatches, it uses the larva of the wasp as a fresh source of food.

**SIZE** ¾ in (1.8–2 cm) long

**DIET** Pollen

**HABITAT** Wasp nests

**DISTRIBUTION** Northern Australia

## Honey bee
*Apis mellifera*

Originally from Southeast Asia, the honey bee is now raised all over the world. It was first domesticated by the ancient Egyptians more than 4,500 years ago.

**SIZE** ½ in (1.2 cm) long

**DIET** Nectar and pollen

**HABITAT** Forests, mountains, grasslands, and urban areas

**DISTRIBUTION** Worldwide

## Horntail
*Urocerus gigas*

Very deceptive in appearance, the horntail does not sting. The "horn" at the end of its abdomen is made up of a harmless spine and an egg-laying tube called an ovipositor. The female uses it to drill holes into pine trees in which to lay her eggs.

**SIZE** 1½ in (3.5–4 cm) long

**DIET** Fungus and wood

**HABITAT** Deciduous and coniferous trees

**DISTRIBUTION** Europe, Asia, northern Africa, and North America

## Wood ant
*Formica rufa*

Wood ants capture aphids and farm them in their nests, milking them by stroking each individual until it releases a drop of sweet honeydew for the ants to feed on. Wood ants spray formic acid if disturbed.

**SIZE** ¼–½ in (8–10 mm) long

**DIET** Honeydew and insects

**HABITAT** Temperate forests

**DISTRIBUTION** Europe and Asia

## Brown jumping spider
*Evarcha arcuata*

Jumping spiders have excellent eyesight. Their eight eyes allow them to sense movement from any direction to avoid predators. Their large, forward-facing eyes allow them to judge distance accurately to pounce on prey. Before leaping, a jumping spider produces a safety line of silk just in case it misses its target.

**SIZE** ¹/₄ in (5–7 mm) long

**DIET** Arthropods

**HABITAT** Grasslands

**DISTRIBUTION** Europe and Asia

## Mexican red-kneed tarantula
*Brachypelma smithi*

Also known as bird-eating spiders, these spiders are large enough to kill small mammals and reptiles with a venomous bite. They use their irritating body hairs in defense.

*Legs are covered in hairs that are sensitive to touch and air movements, helping the spider to sense prey*

**SIZE** 2–3 in (5–7.5 cm) long

**DIET** Mainly large insects

**HABITAT** Tropical deciduous forests

**DISTRIBUTION** Mexico

## Spiny orb-weaver
*Gasteracantha cancriformis*

Its bright and spiny body makes this orb weaver easy to spot. Females spin typically circular webs. Males are much smaller.

**SIZE** Female ¹/₄ in (5–9 mm), male ¹/₁₂–¹/₈ in (2–3 mm) long

**DIET** Insects

**HABITAT** Woodland edges and shrubs

**DISTRIBUTION** Southern United States, Central America, Cuba, and Jamaica

## Common velvet mite
*Trombidium holosericeum*

After a heavy downpour, velvet mites come crawling out of the soil to mate and lay eggs. When young, they live parasitically on other arthropods, such as insects and spiders, but turn predatory as adults. They get their name from the dense, red fur on their bodies.

**SIZE** ¹/₈–¹/₄ in (3–5 mm) long

**DIET** Insect eggs (as adults)

**HABITAT** Tropical forests

**DISTRIBUTION** Europe and Asia

## Imperial scorpion
*Pandinus imperator*

One of the largest scorpions, the imperial scorpion usually stalks its spider prey before grabbing it and crushing it with its claws. The venomous sting at the end of its tail is mainly used for defense.

**SIZE** 6–10 in (15–25 cm) long

**DIET** Spiders, lizards, and small mammals

**HABITAT** Among leaf litter in tropical forests

**DISTRIBUTION** Central and western Africa

*Sting at the tip of the tail*

# Echinoderms

This astonishing array of colorful sea creatures is found only in ocean habitats. Echinoderms' bodies are usually formed from five equal parts arranged in a circle. They have an internal system of water-filled tubes that ends in tube feet, which lets them use water to move and take in oxygen and food.

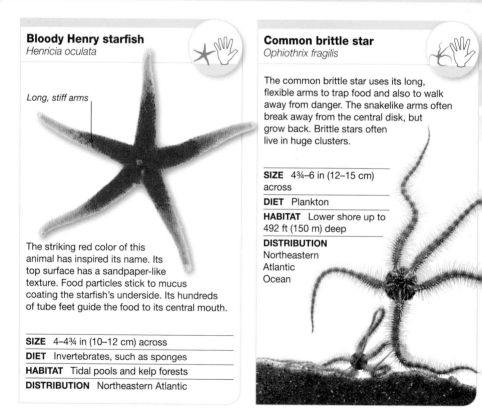

## Bloody Henry starfish
*Henricia oculata*

Long, stiff arms

The striking red color of this animal has inspired its name. Its top surface has a sandpaper-like texture. Food particles stick to mucus coating the starfish's underside. Its hundreds of tube feet guide the food to its central mouth.

| | |
|---|---|
| **SIZE** | 4–4¾ in (10–12 cm) across |
| **DIET** | Invertebrates, such as sponges |
| **HABITAT** | Tidal pools and kelp forests |
| **DISTRIBUTION** | Northeastern Atlantic |

## Common brittle star
*Ophiothrix fragilis*

The common brittle star uses its long, flexible arms to trap food and also to walk away from danger. The snakelike arms often break away from the central disk, but grow back. Brittle stars often live in huge clusters.

| | |
|---|---|
| **SIZE** | 4¾–6 in (12–15 cm) across |
| **DIET** | Plankton |
| **HABITAT** | Lower shore up to 492 ft (150 m) deep |
| **DISTRIBUTION** | Northeastern Atlantic Ocean |

## Yellow sea cucumber
*Colochirus robustus*

Sea cucumbers are soft, tubular animals with a mouth surrounded by food-collecting tentacles. Many sea cucumbers, such as this one, are covered in knobby projections.

**SIZE** 2–3½ in (5–8 cm) long

**DIET** Plankton and decaying organic matter

**HABITAT** Seabed, 26–82 ft (8–25 m) deep

**DISTRIBUTION** Indian Ocean and Pacific Ocean

## Red urchin
*Astropyga radiata*

The hard body covering of the red urchin has long, hollow spines and in between are rows of tube feet, which it uses to walk across the seabed. It is often carried by an urchin crab.

**SIZE** 8 in (20 cm) across

**DIET** Seaweeds, kelp, and algae

**HABITAT** Lagoons

**DISTRIBUTION** Indian Ocean and Pacific Ocean

## Red feather star
*Himerometra robustipinna*

Feather stars are similar to starfish, except their mouth faces upward. They feed on plankton caught by their featherlike arms. Red feather stars are often seen clinging to sponges and corals.

Feathery arm ———

**SIZE** 4–6 in (10–15 cm) across

**DIET** Plankton

**HABITAT** Tropical coastal waters

**DISTRIBUTION** Indian Ocean and Pacific Ocean

# Record breakers

## FASTEST ANIMALS

### ★ Fastest animal on land
A cheetah can run at speeds of up to 70 mph (112 kph) in short bursts, making it the fastest animal on land.

### ★ Fastest speed achieved by a land animal over a long distance
The antelopelike pronghorn of the North American prairies can sustain a speed of 35 mph (56 kph) over a distance of 4 miles (6 km) and 42 mph (67 kph) over a distance of 1 mile (1.6 km).

### ★ Fastest bird in flight
A peregrine falcon can reach speeds of 200 mph (325 kph) when diving—usually to catch prey such as pigeons and doves.

### ★ Fastest bird on land
The ostrich is the fastest bird on land and can run at a speed of 45 mph (73 kph). It is also the biggest bird on land, weighing up to 345 lb (156 kg).

### ★ Fastest fish
The sailfish can swim at speeds of 68 mph (110 kph) in short bursts. It often hunts in groups, shepherding the fish into schools.

### ★ Fastest mammal in water
The Dall's porpoise can surge through water at a speed of 35 mph (56 kph).

### ★ Fastest shark
The world's fastest shark is the mako shark. Estimates of its maximum speed range from 31 mph (50 kph) to 59 mph (95 kph).

## SLOWEST ANIMALS

- **Slugs** are the slowest animals in the world, with a maximum speed of 0.03 mph (0.05 kph).

- **Giant tortoises** are the slowest reptiles on land. Their maximum speed range has been recorded at 0.12–0.3 mph (0.2–0.5 kph). They live longer than most other animals.

- **Seahorses** move by fluttering their dorsal fins. They are the slowest fish, with a recorded speed of 0.0006 mph (0.001 kph).

- **Three-toed sloths** travel at a top speed of 0.15 mph (0.24 kph), making them the slowest land mammals.

- **American woodcocks** are the slowest flying birds, reaching a top speed of just 5 mph (8 kph).

# LARGEST OF ALL

## ♦ Largest animal
The world's largest animal is the blue whale. Females can grow to a length of 89 ft (27 m) and weigh more than 100 tons.

## ♦ Largest animal on land
African savanna elephants are the largest animals on land. The largest elephant known measured 13 ft (4 m) tall at the shoulder and was estimated to weigh more than 22,000 lb (10,000 kg).

## ♦ Largest fish
Whale sharks are longer than many whales. They grow to around 39 ft (12 m) in length.

## ♦ Largest reptile
The saltwater crocodile is 20 ft (6 m) long, making it the largest reptile on the Earth.

## ♦ Largest invertebrate
Colossal squids can reach a length of 43 ft (13 m) and, at 1,090 lb (495 kg), they are the largest invertebrates.

## ♦ Largest invertebrate on land
The coconut crab, or robber crab, has a legspan of 30 in (76 cm). This crustacean climbs palm trees to eat fruit.

## ♦ Largest amphibian
The Chinese giant salamander is the largest amphibian. It can be as long as 6 ft (1.8 m) and can weigh 110 lb (50 kg).

## ♦ Largest wingspan
The wandering albatross has a gigantic wingspan of 11½ ft (3.5 m).

The giant mouth of the world's largest animal, the blue whale, can expand to hold up to 100 tons of food and water.

## ♦ Largest animal colony
An 80-year-old colony of Argentinian ants is spread over 3,750 miles (6,000 km) between Portugal and Italy.

## ♦ Largest structure built by living creatures
Australia's Great Barrier Reef is 1,430 miles (2,300 km) long, covering an area of 133,000 sq miles (344,000 sq km). It is made up of solid remains of countless generations of coral polyps.

## ♦ Largest insect swarm
The largest swarm (group of flying insects) record was of desert locusts in Kenya in 1954. The swarm covered an area of 77 sq miles (200 sq km) with a density of 50 million individuals per 0.39 sq mile (1 sq km), making 10 billion locusts in the swarm.

# LONGEST OF ALL

## ▶ Longest animal
Measuring more than 98½ ft (30 m) in length, the world's longest animals are not blue whales, but a species of ribbon worm.

## ▶ Longest snake
The Asian reticulated python is the longest snake in the world and the longest one on record measured 33 ft (10 m).

## ▶ Longest insect
A newly discovered species of stick insect found in 2008 is the longest insect in the world. Chan's megastick measures 22¼ in (56.7 cm) in length. Its body (excluding the legs) is 14 in (35.7 cm) long.

## ▶ Longest horns
A subspecies of wild water buffalo that lives in India and Myanmar has the longest horns. The record pair measures 3½ ft (1.1 m) from tip to tip.

## ▶ Longest nose
An elephant's trunk can be as long as 8¼ ft (2.5 m). It uses its trunk to smell, to put food in its mouth, and to signal to other elephants.

## ▶ Longest jump by an insect
The froghopper, or spittle bug, is ¼ in (6 mm) long and can hurl itself up to 24 in (61 cm) into the air.

## ▶ Longest arms of any primate
Compared to its body size, a gibbon's arms are the longest among primates. Its arms are around 1.5 times as long as its legs. These tree-dwelling primates use their long arms to swing from one branch to another at high speeds.

A giraffe can grow up to 19 ft (5.8 m) tall, making it the world's tallest animal.

## ▶ Longest fangs
The gaboon viper has the longest fangs of any snake. The average length of the snake is 5 ft (1.5 m) and its fangs can be as long as 2 in (5 cm). The fangs are kept folded against the roof of the snake's mouth.

## ▶ Longest bill
At up to 18½ in (47 cm) long, the bill of the Australian pelican is the longest in the world.

## ▶ Longest tooth
The single tooth, or tusk, of a male narwhal can be as long as 10 ft (3 m). It uses its tusk to defend itself against predators as well as against other males during the mating season.

# LONGEST MIGRATIONS

Many animals undertake long journeys, called migrations, in search of food, or to breed.

## • Longest migration of any animal

Arctic terns fly between the Arctic and the Antarctic every year, covering a round-trip distance of 44,000 miles (70,800 km). They raise chicks in nests in the Arctic tundra, then fly south to avoid the Arctic winter.

## • Longest mammal migration

Gray whales have the longest known migration of any mammal. They travel 10,000–13,000 miles (16,000–21,000 km) every year.

## • Longest nonstop migration

A single bar-tailed godwit (a small wading bird) was tracked during a nonstop flight between Alaska and New Zealand, covering 7,145 miles (11,500 km).

## • Longest insect migration

The monarch butterfly travels around 2,800 miles (4,500 km) every year. However, no individual completes the entire trip. The insects move south from North America to Mexico every fall. In spring they head back north. The females die after laying eggs on the way and new generations continue the journey.

# HEAVIEST OF ALL

### Heaviest flying bird
The great bustard can weigh up to 40 lb (18 kg).

### Heaviest raptor
The average weight of a male Andean condor is 23½ lb (10.7 kg), making it the world's heaviest raptor.

### Heaviest snake
The green anaconda can weigh as much as 220 lb (100 kg), making it the heaviest snake. Its weight can increase by more than half after it has eaten a meal.

# SMALLEST ANIMALS

★ The smallest insect—a type of parasitic wasp called a fairyfly—is 0.004–0.007 in (0.10–0.17 mm) long.

★ *Paedocypris progenetica*, a tiny fish of Indonesian peat swamps, is the world's smallest fish, at just over ¼ in (7.9 mm).

★ The bee hummingbird is the smallest bird. It is 2–2½ in (5–6 cm) in length.

★ The smallest mammal is the bumblebee bat of Thailand. It is 1.1–1¼ in (29–33 mm) long and weighs about 0.07 oz (2 g).

# Glossary

**Antenna** Paired sensory organ on the heads of some invertebrates, such as insects, used to detect vibrations, smells, and tastes.

**Antler** Paired bony growth on the head of deer. Unlike horns, antlers are shed and grow back every year.

**Aquatic** Living or growing in or near water.

**Asexual reproduction** A form of reproduction in which one organism produces offspring without mixing its genes with another parent.

**Baleen** A brushlike fringe that hangs from the upper jaw in some whales. The baleen strains food from water.

**Barbel** Whiskerlike sensory structures around the mouths of some fish, such as catfish, used to find food.

**Beak** A set of protruding jaws made of keratin, usually without teeth. Birds, turtles, and tortoises have beaks.

**Blubber** The thick layer of fat that protects some animals, such as whales and seals, from the cold.

**Camouflage** Colors or patterns on an animal's skin or fur that allow it to blend with its surroundings.

**Carnivore** An animal that eats only meat. It also refers to the mammals in the order Carnivora, such as dogs.

**Carrion** The remains of dead animals.

**Cartilage** A firm, flexible tissue that is part of the skeleton of some vertebrates. In sharks, the entire skeleton is made up of cartilage.

**Cell** The smallest unit in the body of a living organism. It can copy itself to form the different tissues that make up the body of the organism.

**Colony** A group of animals belonging to one species that live together.

**Coniferous** Describes plants, including pine and fir trees, which lack flowers and fruit and produce cones containing their seeds.

**Courtship** Behavior that helps form a bond between a male and a female before mating. It also allows the partners, particularly the female, to assess their potential match and decide whether or not to mate.

**Crustacean** A type of mainly aquatic arthropod with a hard shell and two pairs of antennae.

**Deciduous** Describes trees that shed leaves in the fall and grow new ones in spring.

**Echolocation** One way in which dolphins and bats find their way and locate food. It involves sending out sound signals and then listening for the echoes that bounce back off objects around them.

**Ecosystem** A collection of species living in the same habitat that interact with each other and their environment.

**Ectotherm** An animal that cannot maintain a constant body temperature. Instead, its body temperature varies with its environmental conditions. Also known as cold-blooded. For example, reptiles are cold-blooded and sunbathe to warm up.

**Embryo** An organism in its early stages of development.

**Endangered species** A species that is in danger of becoming extinct, such as the Cuban crocodile.

**Endotherm** An animal that can maintain a constant body temperature internally, using a lot of energy to heat its body or cool it. Also known as warm-blooded.

**Extinct** A species of plant or animal that has died out, such as the Chinese river dolphin.

**Fertilization** The process by which a sex cell from a male joins with one from a female to produce new organisms. It can be internal or external. In external fertilization, the process occurs outside the body of the female.

**Filter feeder** An animal that feeds by taking in large amounts of water with suspended particles of food, which are then strained out of the water.

**Flipper** A paddle-shaped limb of an aquatic mammal or reptile.

**Habitat** The environment in which an animal lives.

**Herbivore** An animal that feeds only on plants or plantlike plankton.

**Hibernation** The ability of some animals to lower their heart rate and body temperature and become inactive during colder months when food is scarce.

**Horn** A structure on the head of some hoofed mammals that is made of a bony core covered with a sheath of keratin.

**Host** An animal on which a parasite feeds.

**Invertebrate** Any animal without a backbone.

**Keel** An enlargement of the breastplate in most birds that anchors the muscles used in flight. The ratites lack this feature.

**Keratin** A tough protein found in hair, nails, claws, hooves, and horns.

**Larva** The immature, often wormlike, form that hatches from the eggs of many insects and other invertebrates.

**Mantle** The body wall of a mollusk. In shelled mollusks, it builds up the shell. It is made up of a fold of skin that protects the internal organs.

**Marine** Found in the sea.

**Metamorphosis** A major change in an animal's body shape during its life cycle. Caterpillars turn into butterflies or moths through metamorphosis.

**Migration** A journey undertaken by an animal due to seasonal changes, usually to find food or to breed.

**Nymph** An early stage of development of an invertebrate that generally looks and lives in the same way as the organism's adult form.

**Omnivore** An animal that eats both plants and animals.

**Pack** A group of animals that hunt together.

**Parasite** An animal that lives on, or inside, the body of another species, known as the host. It feeds on the host animal or on food the host has swallowed. It has a harmful effect on the host.

**Pigment** A substance that colors the tissues of an organism.

**Placenta** The organ inside the womb of many female mammals that allows exchange of nutrients and waste between the mother and developing young.

**Plankton** The mass of tiny aquatic microorganisms and animals that are eaten by larger animals.

**Predator** An animal that hunts, kills, and eats other animals.

**Prey** An animal that is hunted, killed, and eaten by a predator.

**Protein** A type of complex chemical found in all life-forms.

**Pupa** The stage in the life cycle of certain insects in which the larva is protected by a special case as it metamorphoses into the adult form.

**Rainforest** Dense tropical woodland that receives heavy rainfall.

**Scales** Plates that protect the skin of most fish and some reptiles.

**Scavenger** An animal, such as a vulture, that feeds on the remains of dead animals or plants.

**Spawning** The process in which an animal produces or deposits eggs. Spawning is common in water-dwelling animals.

**School** A large group of fish moving as one.

**Species** A group of organisms that breed only with each other.

**Talons** The sharp claws of a bird of prey.

**Thorax** The middle section of an insect's body. It bears the legs and wings.

**Temperate** Relating to the region of the world between the tropical and polar regions that is neither extremely hot nor very cold.

**Territory** An area occupied by an animal or group of animals from which other members of the same species are excluded. Territories are usually defended from other members but sometimes only during the breeding season.

**Troop** A gathering of one kind of primate, such as monkeys.

**Tropical** Relating to the hot region of the world spanning the equator, between the tropics of Cancer and Capricorn.

**Vertebrate** Any animal with a backbone.

**Wingspan** The measurement from the tip of one wing of a bird or insect to that of the other when the wings are outstretched.

# Index

## AB

# Acknowledgments

Dorling Kindersley would like to thank: Monica Byles for proofreading; Helen Peters for indexing; David Roberts and Rob Campbell for database creation; Claire Bowers, Fabian Harry, Romaine Werblow, and Rose Horridge for DK Picture Library assistance; and Shatarupa Chaudhuri for editorial assistance.

**The publishers would also like to thank the following for their kind permission to reproduce their photographs:**

(Key: a-above; b-below/bottom; c-center; f-far; l-left; r-right; t-top)

**2–3 Dorling Kindersley:** Thomas Marent (c). **4 Dorling Kindersley:** Jan Van Der Voort (c). **5 Corbis:** Tim Laman / National Geographic Society (c). **6 Alamy Images:** Marko König / imagebroker (bc). **Dorling Kindersley:** Jerry Young (tr). **Getty Images:** Tony Tilford / Oxford Scientific (br). **7 Dorling Kindersley:** Mike Danzenbaker (tc, cra); Natural History Museum, London (tr); Jerry Young (cla, cl, crb). **Getty Images:** Pam Francis / Photographer's Choice (tl, ca, c). **9 Dorling Kindersley:** Peter Minister, Digital Sculptor (tr). **Getty Images:** Chris Mattison / Photographer's Choice (tc). **10 Alamy Images:** Ville Palonen (r). **11 Corbis:** Bob Krist (cr). **12 FLFA:** Gerry Ellis / Minden Pictures. **14 Corbis:** Mick Roessler (b). **15 Corbis:** Tom Brakefield (b). **Dorling Kindersley:** Jerry Young (tc). **16 Corbis:** Leonard Lee Rue III / Visuals Unlimited (tl); Frank Lukasseck / Terra (cl); Ronald Wittek / dpa (bl). **Dorling Kindersley:** Jerry Young (br). **17 Dorling Kindersley:** Booth Museum of Natural History, Brighton (bl). **18 Dorling Kindersley:** Jerry Young (br). **Alamy Images:** Arco Images / Therin-Weise (tc/Anteater); Ivan Kuzmin (tl). **Corbis:** Michael & Patricia Fogden (cl). **FLPA:** Derek Middleton (br). **Getty Images:** Nigel Dennis / age fotostock (tr). **20–21 Fotolia:** Eric Isselée (b). **20 FLPA:** Richard Du Toit / Minden Pictures (tl). **21 FLPA:** Frans Lanting (br). **22 Dorling Kindersley:** Jerry Young (br). **Getty Images:** Martin Harvey / Gallo Images (cl); Oxford Scientific (tl, bl). **23 Dorling Kindersley:** Natural History Museum, London (bl). **24 Dorling Kindersley:** Jerry Young (br). **26–27 Photolibrary:** Juan Carlos Munoz / Age Fotostock. **30 Corbis:** Ocean (bl); W. Perry Conway (cl). **31 Dorling Kindersley:** Jerry Young (bl). **32–33 Dorling Kindersley:** Philip Dowell (bc). **34–35 FLPA:** Jurgen & Christine

Sohns. **36 Dorling Kindersley:** Dudley Edmonson (l). **37 Dreamstime.com:** Morten Hilmer (tr). **39 Getty Images:** Michael Fay / National Geographic (br). **41 Corbis:** Karen Kasmauski / Science Faction (tl); Ocean (c). **46 Dorling Kindersley:** Thomas Marent. **47 Corbis:** Kevin Schafer (bc). **48–49 Getty Images:** Berndt Fischer / Oxford Scientific (t). **48 Dorling Kindersley:** Natural History Museum, London (br, br/Tail feathers, br). **50 Dorling Kindersley:** Twycross Zoo, Atherstone, Leicestershire (br). **51 Corbis:** Macduff Everton / Terra (tr); Steven Vidler / Eurasia Press (tc). **54 Dorling Kindersley:** Dudley Edmondson (br). **56 Dorling Kindersley:** Mike Lane (cr); Robert Royse. **61 Dorling Kindersley:** Brian E. Small (bl). **Photolibrary:** Photodisc / Tom Brakefield (tr). **62 Corbis:** W. Perry Conway (cl). **Dorling Kindersley:** Brian E. Small (br). **64–65 Photolibrary:** SMuller. **66 Dorling Kindersley:** David Tipling Photo Library (br); Tomi Muukonen (bl). **67 Dorling Kindersley:** Anders Paulsrud (tl); Markus Varesvuo (tl); Sean Hunter Photography (r). **69 Corbis:** Jochen Schlenker / Robert Harding World Imagery (tl). **Getty Images:** Greg Wood / AFP (tc). **70 Alamy Images:** Michael P. L. Fogden / Bruce Coleman Inc. (tl). **Corbis:** Radius Images (cl). **Dorling Kindersley:** Melvin Grey (br). **71 Dorling Kindersley:** Mike Danzenbaker (b); Barry Hughes (tr). **72 Dorling Kindersley:** Brian E. Small (br); Jari Peltomaki (b). **74 Corbis:** Joe Petersburger / National Geographic Society (b). **75 Dorling Kindersley:** Mike Read (b). **76 Dorling Kindersley:** Dudley Edmondson (tr); Jerry Young (br). **77 Getty Images:** Nacivet / Photographer's Choice. **78 Dorling Kindersley:** Thomas Marent. **79 Getty Images:** Anup Shah / The Image Bank (bc). **80 Corbis:** Jack Goldfarb / Design Pics (cl). **81 Corbis:** Joe McDonald (tl). **Getty Images:** Jack Milchanowsk / age fotostock (r). **83 Dorling Kindersley:** Jerry Young (bl). **88 Corbis:** Joe McDonald (tl). **Getty Images:** Visuals Unlimited (cr). **90 Dorling Kindersley:** Thomas Marent. **91 Corbis:** Visuals Unlimited (bc). **93 Corbis:** Visuals Unlimited (tr). **96–97 FLPA:** Emanuele Biggi (tl). **98 Dorling Kindersley:** Jerry Young (tl). **Photoshot:** NHPA (bl). **102 FLPA:** Chris Newbert. **104 Corbis:** Gary Meszaros / Visuals Unlimited (bc). **105 Alamy Images:** David Fleetham (cr). **Corbis:** Tim Davis (bl); Visuals Unlimited (tc); Norbert Wu / Science Faction (tr). **Getty Images:** Frank & Joyce Burek / Photodisc (bc). **106 Alamy Images:** blickwinkel / Hartl (b). **107**

**Getty Images:** Peter Scoones / Taxi (t). **Oceanwidelmages.com:** (b). **108 Corbis:** image100 (br). **Getty Images:** Ann & Steve Toon / Robert Harding World Imagery (tr). **109 Corbis:** Norbert Wu / Science Faction (tr). **Dorling Kindersley:** Peter M Forster (bl). **110 Corbis:** Norbert Wu / Science Faction (tl). **113 Dorling Kindersley:** Linda Pitkin / lindapitkin.net (t). **114–115 Alamy Images:** shapencolour. **116 Dorling Kindersley:** Luc Viatour (tl); Weymouth Sea Life Centre (bl). **118 Dorling Kindersley:** Thomas Marent. **119 Getty Images:** Danita Delimont / Gallo Images (bc). **120 Corbis:** Ocean (cr). **Dorling Kindersley:** Linda Pitkin / lindapitkin.net (cl). **121 Corbis:** Nigel Cattlin / Visuals Unlimited (b). **122 Dorling Kindersley:** Linda Pitkin / lindapitkin.net (bl). **124 Dorling Kindersley:** Linda Pitkin / lindapitkin.net (cl). **124–125 Dorling Kindersley:** Linda Pitkin / lindapitkin.net (bc). **125 Alamy Images:** Peter Wirtz / F1online digitale Bildagentur GmbH (tr). **Corbis:** George Grall / National Geographic Society (tc). **NHPA / Photoshot:** Paul Kay (tl). **126 FLPA:** Reinhard Dirscherl (br). **130 Dorling Kindersley:** Geoff Brightling / Staab Studios - modelmakers (br). **131 Alamy Images:** Mira (cl). **Dorling Kindersley:** Natural History Museum, London (tr). **Dreamstime.com:** Jefras (tl). **Oceanwidelmages.com:** (cr). **133 Dorling Kindersley:** Linda Pitkin / lindapitkin.net (br). **imagequestmarine.com:** (tr). **134 Dorling Kindersley:** Natural History Museum, London (tl). **135 Dorling Kindersley:** Martin Heigan (tl). **136–137 Dorling Kindersley:** Thomas Marent. **138 Dorling Kindersley:** Jerry Young (tr, br). **140 Dorling Kindersley:** Natural History Museum, London (tc, br). **141 Dorling Kindersley:** Booth Museum of Natural History, Brighton (bl). **145 Dorling Kindersley:** Linda Pitkin / lindapitkin.net (tl, tr).

**Jacket images:** *Front:* **Dorling Kindersley:** Dudley Edmonson tc/ (Arctic Fox), Natural History Museum, London tc, tc/ (Cicada), Paignton Zoo, Devon tr/ (giraffe), Weymouth Sea Life Centre tr, Jerry Young ca, cla; **Getty Images:** Photodisc / Keren Su bc, JH Pete Carmichael / The Image Bank c; *Spine:* **Getty Images:** JH Pete Carmichael / The Image Bank t.

All other images © Dorling Kindersley

For further information see: www.dkimages.com